MEMORY

MEMORY

How we use it, lose it and can improve it

DAVID SAMUEL

Weidenfeld & Nicolson
LONDON

First published in Great Britain in 1999
by Weidenfeld & Nicolson

A CIP catalogue record for this book
is available from the British Library.

ISBN 0 297 81837 6

Printed and bound in Great Britain by
Butler & Tanner Ltd, Frome and London

Weidenfeld & Nicolson
The Orion Publishing Group Ltd
Orion House
5 Upper Saint Martin's Lane
London, WC2H 9EA

This book is dedicated to my wife, Eve Black,
without whose skills, constant encouragement
and very wise advice, this would never
have been written.

CONTENTS

PREFACE

The scientific understanding of memory has undergone a major revolution in the past decade. Although the interpretation of the phenomenon, in material terms, has fascinated everyone from philosophers in ancient times to scientists from all disciplines today – 'learning and memory' have come of age. This may be due either to a daring new approach to the subject or, more likely, to the final emergence of a fascinating new discipline of science, following recent developments in both understanding and technology.

Research on the brain and nervous system, officially called neuroscience, has now reached the status of a recognized discipline – on a par with physics, chemistry and biology – and is now a legitimate and prestigious area of investigation. Only a few years ago, research on learning and memory was considered just a 'collection of correlations'. There was even difficulty in distinguishing between the possible, the probable and the certain – the characteristics of 'woolly' science. This sudden acceptance has, sadly enough, been partly brought about by the scourge of Alzheimer's disease, which has pressured government departments as well as professional scientists, pharmaceutical companies, and even faculties of the sciences and the humanities, to acknowledge research on memory, its loss and recovery, as a respectable occupation. As a result, there has been in the past few years a torrent of experimental data and ideas about the nature of memory. In addition, particularly in hard-line, professional scientific circles, which include physical chemists, physicists, molecular and cell biologists, and even mathematicians, research on memory is now accepted, due to the efforts of 'memory modellers'. These are a pioneer band of computer specialists who are trying, with slow but increasing success, to determine the shortest chain of biochemical events in the brain, which are required to explain the twin phenomena of learning and memory. It has taken over 3000 years from the first vague suggestions by philosophers and dreamers to the acceptance of memory as a legitimate scientific discipline, due to a combination of an intense interest in a few neurological diseases, the development of novel scientific approaches, new technologies, and the emergence of computers fast enough to deal with complicated chains of events.

This book will describe the aspects of memory that we now understand. It will mention many of the false leads and erroneous assumptions made along the way, but will mainly describe and explain what is known today. Many tens of thousands of scientists are now active in this field. Their work is increasingly sophisticated and often difficult to understand, but in this book I will seek to present the basis of the current theories and their relevant facts. Brain research is a very dynamic field. The key concepts are being confirmed, the major enigmas unravelled and the main players universally recognized. New discoveries are being made daily; every effort has been made to bring what is known about memory up to date and to convey the aura of excitement pervading the field.

ACKNOWLEDGEMENTS

I am most grateful to all my colleagues and students, both in Israel and abroad, for many discussions on 'matters of the brain', which nourished my interest in memory. It also gives me great pleasure to acknowledge the influence of two people in formulating the ideas and opinions contained in this book. First, Professor David Krech, of the Department of Psychology at the University of California, Berkeley, introduced me to the challenges and subtleties of psychology when I was on sabbatical in California during the turbulent 1960s and, second, my grandfather, Herbert Louis, first Viscount Samuel, a philosopher and statesman, instilled in me a spirit of inquiry and an insistence on accuracy both of which I have tried to maintain throughout this book.

CHAPTER ONE

What is memory?

'Tell me where is fancie bread – or in the heart or in the head?'
Portia in *The Merchant of Venice* (William Shakespeare, 1564–1616)

Memory is a difficult word to define, although most people have what appears to an instinctive definition from an early age. Small children have, no doubt, been taught what the word means by their parents, grandparents and teachers. Without needing a precise definition, research on memory now occupies the time of thousands of scientists and students working all over the world. They are part of an enormous enterprise known generally as brain research but more accurately as the neurosciences. The neurosciences are a newly emerging discipline, comparable with other sciences that emerged, like computer or environmental sciences from other disciplines. Computer sciences are a giant offspring born from mathematics in the 1940s and 1950s, whereas environmental sciences more recently evolved from geology and oceanography. The neurosciences were born from a number of disciplines ranging from psychology, animal and human behaviour, to chemistry, biology, physics and mathematics. Those working on memory are now agreed that the word refers to 'the systems, representations and processes in living organisms that are involved in the retention of information', but this is a rather clumsy definition.

Being a rather bookish person, I have always had great faith in dictionaries, since lexicographers have spent years worrying about the meaning of words, and have, no doubt, consulted all the experts, books and other possible sources of information. All major dictionaries include a wide list of alternatives under the definition of memory. Among these are 'the mental faculty of retaining and recalling past experience' and perhaps better, 'the ability to keep things in mind and recall them at will'. The latter reminds one of a balancing act by a juggler, keeping six balls in the air at once. However, the memory of even the simplest, multicellular creature is not a matter of chance or skill, but is a well-organized and extremely complicated system, determined fundamentally by the genes and by experience. Human memory is a highly developed and extremely efficient system, as we shall see in the following six chapters. As defined by dictionaries, memory means not only 'the act of remembering', but also 'the person, thing, happening or act remembered'. In addition, some definitions include the element of time, such as the 'period covered by the remembrance of a person or group. Other definitions include the use of the words 'from memory' to mean that something is remembered without the aid of notes, and the expression 'in memory of', meaning in honour of a certain person after their death.

This list indicates that there is considerable ambiguity in the use of the word 'memory' and its relationship to learning. In fact, learning and memory were for decades semantic twins. These terms are still used throughout the neurosciences, but purists now emphasize the 'plasticity' of the brain, meaning the initial or changing part of the process of remembering. This book will not discuss any of the newer applications of the word 'memory', such as computer memory, the storage capacity of a computer, or the fact that certain materials and metals have a 'memory' that can return them to a previous shape after deformation. One example is a steel spring. Better examples are certain alloys – that is, mixtures of metals – that have different shapes at different temperatures. This 'metallic shape memory' has many technological applications, but we will not go into them here.

Memory is not only a store, but has a number of curious features that will be discussed in more detail in this book. First, as we have already seen, it is related to learning. Learning is defined as the acquisition of knowledge, comprehension, ability or skill, either purposefully or accidentally. In other words, it is the accumulation of information by studying, experience or instruction. This accumulation is usually called 'input', and I shall discuss some of the ways it occurs via the senses in Chapter 3.

An important feature of memory, or of the process of remembering, is recall or recollecting at will. 'At will' is an interesting point, since learning is not usually automatic but involves attention, concentration and effort. A good or a bad memory, in the singular, is an important part of everyone's life. Memories of pleasant or unpleasant things are often called 'good' or 'bad' memories. The differences between these rather sloppily named concepts will be dealt with later. What we call a 'good' memory varies from individual to individual. It has, in fact, become one of the main preoccupations of students and the major concern of people growing old. People who complain about having a poor or bad memory usually mean their fading ability to recall things. As in learning, the question can be asked: how much of the process of recall is deliberate and how much is instinctive or automatic; and, of course, what can one do to improve it? The opposite of remembering is usually called forgetting. An important, still open question in psychology is: can one 'learn to forget', and if not, why not?

The common definitions of the word 'forget' include 'to put out of one's mind', meaning the active or intentional overlooking of an object, an insult and so on. As Groucho Marx, the great comic actor, is said to have remarked, 'I never forget a face, but in your case I am willing to make an exception.' Finally, there is the odd phrase 'to forget oneself', meaning to lose control or behave without suitable dignity, which I shall not discuss any further.

The simple concept of input, storage and recall or retrieval, known as memory, has concerned a wide range of people from the philosophers of ancient times to the cognitive psychologists, neurologists, chemists, biologists, physicists, psychiatrists and computer experts of today. Curiously, although the Bible is full of concern for memory in the form of admonitions to remember and not to forget, there is no concern with what actually occurs. During their forty years in the desert, the children of Israel are described as remembering the good times that they thought they had had in Egypt. They were also constantly exhorted not to forget the Holy Sabbath (the fourth commandment), to remember the feast of Passover and to remember to offer sacrifices on certain occasions. The processes of remembering and forgetting, however, are never discussed. The first mention of the transience of memory *per se* in the Bible is in Genesis. Here the story is told of how the chief baker in Pharaoh's court, who was thrown into prison, did not remember Joseph – once a prince and now a fellow prisoner. It is said in the Bible that the baker 'did not remember Joseph but forgat (sic) him'. How or why he forgot is not discussed, but it helped Joseph to get released. The brain as such is never mentioned in the Bible. In fact, the word used is believed to refer to bone marrow, and it is suggested that emotions or brain functions are located in the kidneys or the bowels.

The Greeks, on the other hand, were much concerned with the function of the brain in general and its relationship to memory. As far as we know, the wise men in very ancient civilizations, in Egypt, Assyria and Babylon, all thought that the heart was the seat of intelligence and emotion. A much quoted, more recent example is the perhaps apocryphal comment by a Native American to the psychoanalyst and philosopher, C.J. Jung: 'I know that you white men think with the brain. That accounts for your shortcomings. We red men think with the heart.' Even the early Chinese did not connect the brain with perception or thought, until the Middle Ages, when Jesuit missionaries brought in European ideas of the role of the brain and merged them with the prevailing Chinese philosophy.

Among the ancient Greek philosophers there is an interesting see-saw of ideas about the emotions, and the location of the senses. There was also much concern with the origin of pain and epilepsy, in order to be able to alleviate or cure them. Various bizarre treatments and even incantations were used to deal with pain, and many famous men in those times seem to have suffered from epilepsy, which could not be cured. The earliest Greek philosophers, living before the Socratic age, around the sixth century BC, were probably the first to suggest that everything within the universe operates according to fixed laws that could eventually be understood by careful reasoning.

During the following three or four centuries, centres of philosophy, mathematics and medicine were established around the eastern Mediterranean to study the various components of nature and its laws. Each centre usually revolved around a singular, dominant personality, surrounded by scholars who carried on his tradition. Whenever the interaction between philosophers and physicians was strong, more advanced ideas on the role of the brain and, indirectly, of the senses and memory were suggested. The Pythagorean brotherhood, for example, not only were concerned with geometry, but interacted with the ancient medical school in Croton in southern Italy and, indeed, suggested that the brain was the site of sensation, vision and perhaps memory. This concept was developed by other pre-Socratic philosophers, notably Democritus, about 400 BC, better known as the originator of the idea of atoms, i.e. particles of matter. He even had the original idea that atoms were more numerous in the brain than elsewhere, hence the supremacy of this organ. But there remained a school of thought in ancient Greece that blood was the medium of thought and that the degree of intelligence depended on its composition.

The Hippocratic school for the teaching and practice of medicine, which flourished on the Greek island of Kos, off the coast of Turkey, in the fifth century BC, was the first to associate epilepsy (known then as the Sacred Disease) with the brain. They considered the brain to be the source not only of feelings and emotions, but also of madness. The understanding of human anatomy among the Hippocratic school was very superficial, since they did not practice dissection. However, to their credit, they rejected the supernatural causes of mental disorders, and suggested that epilepsy was not sacred or of divine origin. They considered that the brain might be the focus of this disease and did, at least, describe the symptoms of epilepsy accurately.

Regarding the brain, the Hippocratic school considered that

it ought to be generally known that the source of our pleasure, merriment, laughter, and amusement, as of our grief, pain, anxiety, and tears, is none other than the brain. It is specially the organ which enables us to think, see, and hear, and to distinguish the ugly and the beautiful, the bad and the good, pleasant and unpleasant ... It is the brain, too, which is the seat of madness and delirium, of the fears and frights which assail us, often by night, but sometimes even by day; it is there where lies the cause of insomnia and sleep-walking, of thoughts that will not come, forgotten duties, and eccentricities.

Furthermore, they wrote that neither the heart nor the diaphragm is involved in mental operations, which are undertaken by the brain.

A retrograde step in the understanding of the predominant role of the brain in mental function and memory, is attributed to Aristotle, who, although born to a family of physicians in 384 BC, spent many years in Plato's more philosophical Academy in Athens. At a very early age he was appointed as a private tutor to the young Alexander the Great, and therefore was a man of considerable importance. He did suggest, on purely theoretical grounds, that all animals and humans had a heart–brain system in which the brain had a minor role. However, he stated unequivocally that the brain is not responsible for any sensation such as pleasure or pain, and is not involved in movement. He considered that the major function of the brain was to cool the blood – like a radiator in a car's cooling system, in modern-day terminology. He suggested that the relatively large size of the human brain, as compared to that of other animals, is due to the necessity of cooling the hot blood of such superior beings, but that the brain itself remained 'cold and wet'. In his defence, it must be said that Aristotle considered that higher mental functions, such as memory, imagination and reason, were not located in the heart or in any particular part of the body.

The Roman statesman Cicero (106–43 BC) chronicled many of these early Greek ideas in his book, *On Oratory: The Art of Debate and Argument*. He discussed memory and wrote that both Plato and Aristotle likened memory, wherever it was located, to a wax tablet (*tabula rasa*) upon which new memories were inscribed. This much-quoted metaphor of a wax tablet does not, however, explain very much except that the brain is blank at birth, which is, of course, not strictly true, and that memories are slowly accumulated by inscription on the wax, and later for some reason gradually fade.

A great step forward in understanding the role of the brain was taken by the Greek philosophers associated with the great museum (i.e. university) at Alexandria, founded at the end of the fourth century BC. It has been suggested that the close proximity to Egyptian physicians and embalmers helped remove the inhibitions of the Greek scholars to a systematic study of the anatomy of both humans and animals. The conclusion was reached that the brain played a dominant role in sensation, thought and movement.

This view was developed through the following centuries, particularly by the physician Galen (*c.* AD 200), who was born in Pergamon, Asia Minor, and educated in Alexandria, and who became the court physician to the emperors in Rome. He studied the effects of head and spine injuries on the movement and behaviour of wounded gladiators, which again emphasized the central role of the brain and nervous system in motion, vision and behaviour in general. Galen confirmed many of these ideas by experiments on piglets, thereby introducing a novel, experimental approach to his work. He also introduced the concept of 'softness', which he claimed was different in each part of the human brain, and also suggested that intellect, thought and even the soul were associated with the central nervous system. Galen did not specifically link memory with any part of the brain, but suggested that the ventricles – the liquid-filled hollow spaces within it – had a major role, and that thoughts and other mental processes are localized in these liquids rather than in solid brain tissue.

This idea appealed to the early Christian Church fathers in the fourth and fifth centuries. St Augustine (AD 354–430), for instance, was convinced that sensory perception (i.e. vision) reason and even memory were located in different ventricles. There was disagreement among these early theologians about which ventricle was associated with which function, but the general concept was accepted for over a thousand years. It was only when natural philosophers, i.e. early scientists, returned to dissection and experimentation that the 'ventricular theory' was eventually abandoned.

One of these natural philosophers was Leonardo da Vinci (1452–1519), an outstanding anatomist, artist, engineer and inventor, who made casts of the ventricles of animals, mainly oxen. He pointed out that the ventricles did not vary much in relative size across species, in spite of an obvious difference in intellect between, say, an ox and a man. This shook the foundations of the ventricular dogma. At about the same time, both the Arab and Jewish philosopher-physicians of the Middle Ages had become convinced of the major role of the brain in thought and emotion.

In the seventeenth century, René Descartes (1596–1650), a dominant figure in mathematics and philosophy, produced a mechanical explanation for the function of the brain. He was particularly interested in the role of the pineal gland. His reasoning was based on the erroneous idea that there was no pineal in animals – hence their relative weakness in intellectual abilities. He also suggested that, since there is only one pineal gland, centrally located in a symmetrical brain – two hemispheres that are mirror images of one another – it must be the 'seat of the soul'. The importance of the pineal, he believed, was as a sort of gateway for the flow of liquid from the ventricles on one side to those on the other. This mechanical, or rather hydraulic, model had no experimental support whatsoever, but fitted in well with the fashion for explaining everything in mechanical terms. This approach – explanation by analogy – has been in vogue ever since, and was the start of a whole series of models of the brain which have lasted until today. Following the hydraulic model, there was the electric model, the computer model and the hologram model, none of which satisfactorily explained the phenomenon of memory.

Returning to history, a number of scientists, philosophers and physicians contributed to our understanding of the workings of the brain in general, and of memory in particular. Among the scientists was Luigi Galvani in Bologna, at the end of the eighteenth century, who discovered animal electricity in frogs' legs. His actual experiment showed that the dissected legs of frogs twitched when connected to an electricity-generating machine. This indicated that bioelectricity was somehow related to the neuromuscular system: that is, the connection between the nervous system and the muscles. These ideas eventually opened up the whole field of electrophysiology, which was developed most brilliantly by Lord Adrian in the 1930s at Cambridge, and which is today one of the mainstays of research on the brain, particularly movement and vision, and to some extent memory.

Three seventeenth- and eighteenth-century philosophers had a great impact on the understanding of the brain. John Locke (1632–1704), in England, suggested that the body gains 'experience' through the senses – for the 'mind' to store and use. He thereby raised the problem of the separate existence of mind and brain that has bedevilled philosophers ever since, and which will be discussed in Chapter 7. He was followed by the Scot, James Stuart Mill (1773–1836), who suggested that the mind (in this case, the brain) is a machine that can be explained in physical terms. He partially reinforced the Greek idea that there is nothing magical or illogical in the way the brain and, by implication, memory work. Finally, the German philosopher Immanuel Kant (1724–1804) was probably the first to distinguish between innate and acquired knowledge – an important distinction that will enter the discussion at various points throughout this book.

An important landmark in the study of the brain was the observation by the Spaniard, Santiago Ramon y Cajal, at the beginning of the twentieth century, that the brain contains millions of minute cells, neurons, connected by long, thread-like processes (see Chapter 2). From this developed the crucial idea that brain cells are connected by means of these processes at junctions called 'synapses', which are like toll gates on a road system. The control of the movement of vehicles along these roads is actually undertaken by chemical processes at the 'toll gates', as will be discussed later. This big breakthrough in the understanding of the action of the brain is due to Charles Scott Sherrington, a British neurophysiologist who, in the 1920s, put forward the idea that there is a web of connections in the brain, much like an old-fashioned telephone exchange in which the plugs represent the bridging synapses. He saw the brain as an 'enchanted loom', in which the bioelectric currents weave an intricate pattern that represents many of the brain's functions.

Among those who can be considered to be the founding fathers of brain and memory research are two Russians. At the beginning of the twentieth century, Ivan Pavlov, in St Petersburg, was one of the earliest physiologists to investigate the basic rules of learning. As most people know, he trained dogs to salivate at the sound of a bell paired with food. He then showed that, with repetition, they would salivate merely at the sound of the bell – without the food. This process of learning is now referred to as a conditioned reflex, but of course it involves memory.

Another Russian neuroscientist, Alexander Lurie, is perhaps less known but equally important for his studies during the 1920s, 1930s and 1940s of memory in humans. As a neurosurgeon, he studied many unusual cases – mostly brain-damaged patients with various defects caused by injuries. He was also involved with a man named S., who had a prodigious memory and who, after seeing extremely complicated arithmetic problems for only a few minutes, could remember them fifty years later.

S., or Shereskevskii to give him his real name, was able to perform many such feats, described by Lurie in his book *The Mind of a Mnemonist* (a rememberer). Sadly enough, S. later became a music-hall entertainer, displaying feats of memory, and died in obscurity. There have since been a number of such people with unusually good memories, such as Dominic O'Brien, who in the 1993 World Memory Championships could remember over 1000 different numbers after studying a list for only thirty minutes. The way these mnemonists succeed in doing this is still not fully understood. The earliest, probably apocryphal example is Simonides, whose feats and method will be discussed in Chapter 4.

Two Canadians have also been major contributors to the study of memory. Wilder Penfield was a neurosurgeon at the Montreal Neurological Institute, and studied the memories of many of his thousand or so patients in the 1950s. Most of these were epileptics, who underwent fairly successful surgery to cure their symptoms. A famous case was the patients H.M., who underwent a very drastic treatment for epilepsy, consisting of the removal of some critically important parts of his brain. These included two-thirds of his hippocampus, a brain region named from the Latin for a sea-horse, which has, with some imagination, the same shape. H.M.'s failure to remember certain specific things following the operation showed that the hippocampus is a vital link in most types of memory. During the following fifty years, many other patients in different countries, with specific damage to the brain caused by bullets, pickaxes, crowbars, etc., and designated for ethical reasons only by their initials, have been the mainstay of brain research in general, and memory in particular.

In the 1950s, Penfield was also responsible for an extremely important discovery. In the course of his many operations, he found that by gently stimulating given regions of the brain of anaesthetized, epileptic patients with an electric probe, he could elicit certain functions such as movement of limbs, visions of well-remembered scenes, and even the hearing of music and human voices. In this way, he was able to produce a detailed map of the functions of various regions in the brain. These maps have been confirmed by work in animals, mainly rats and monkeys with much simpler nervous systems. Deliberate, accurately located lesions were made in animal brains to enable such maps to be made more accurately.

The exact mechanisms by which the five senses (vision, touch, taste, smell and hearing) are processed in the brain is today a very active field of research, as will be discussed in Chapter 3.

The second Canadian was the psychologist Donald Hebb (at McGill University), who at about the same time advanced the idea that learning is due to the facilitation of certain synapses (pathways), thereby laying down a route through the brain which leads to memory. How and why this is believed to occur will be discussed in Chapter 4.

Also around this time, the psychologist Karl Lashley in the United States, using the lesion technique in an attempt to find the seat of memory, studied maze learning in rats. By making cuts in various areas of their brains, he hoped to find the location, or 'engram' as he called it, for memory. To his great dismay he could not find any area which, when destroyed, disrupted learning or memory, and eventually published a classic paper, 'In search of the engram', in which he concluded, somewhat cynically, that he might have proved that memory simply did not exist. This important discovery showed that the study of memory is not easy and that only by studying the whole brain and the interaction between its various parts can any headway be made.

Learning is inseparable from memory, but it is also not easy to define. It is essential for the survival of all creatures, from simple multicellular organisms in the sea to humans. Learning is a crucial activity of all societies – it is the basis, in fact, of all cultures – enabling humans to adapt themselves to live together. It has even enabled modern anthro-pologists to learn to live in the stone-age world of primitive tribes in New Guinea or the upper Amazon, without too much hardship. Learning is also involved in enabling astronauts to overcome the weightlessness of an orbiting space station. In general, humans must constantly acquire new skills and knowledge in order to survive as well as to be accepted among their fellows. People have to learn norms of behaviour at an early age and later to accept other peoples, prejudices and beliefs. Neurobiologists have named this adaptability 'plasticity', which consists of learning and memory as one continuous process.

Primitive organisms such as worms and flies have a limited range of learning, mainly in order to find nourishment, to avoid discomfort and to reproduce. Humans, at the other end of the scale, devote much of their time, particularly during their early years, learning to do nearly everything – walk, talk, reason, etc. In fact, in adult life humans spend more time learning than actually doing things. For this purpose, they have created institutions from schools to universities, as well as methods and techniques for acquiring knowledge – some for survival and some purely for pleasure.

It should be noted, however, that not all changes in behaviour are learned. There are, in fact, two ways in which animals and humans can survive by adapting to changes in the environment. One is 'in the genes', for those behavioural traits that increase the chances for survival. The altered genes, which give an extra advantage are then passed from generation to generation as part of their genetic endowment. This is, as Darwin and others have pointed out, a very slow process taking many generations. The second method of adaptation to the environment is to learn – a process that is far quicker. These two forms of adaptation are popularly known as 'nature' and 'nurture'.

There has been a great deal of discussion during the past hundred years or so as to what extent behaviours are inherited (ie. passed on in the genes), and to what extent they are learned. A very basic example of gene-borne behaviour is the reflex. Human babies are born with a sucking reflex, i.e. an automatic sucking motion that is activated when the infant's mouth is placed near to the nipple. On the other hand, babies are born unable to walk, to talk meaningfully or to look after themselves. All these need guidance or instruction, usually from parents or minders, and later from teachers.

Horses stand up, stagger and then run within hours of being born. They can soon look after themselves, but never learn to talk. However, there is a well-known story of a horse named 'Clever Hans', who toured the Continent with his trainer, giving the answers to simple arithmetic by tapping his hoof to a given number. There is some debate about how Clever Hans was able to do this. Some say it was outright fraud, while others have suggested that the horse looked for almost invisible signs or clues from his trainer. Be that as it may, it seems unlikely that horses can do arithmetic, although they probably have a 'feeling' for simple numbers. Birds can tell how many eggs are in their nests, although often not accurately enough to detect an extra one laid there by a cuckoo.

Learning and memory in many living creatures is often hard to distinguish from innate behaviour or even chance.

An important feature of learning is that it takes time – it is usually not instantaneous. This means that there is a period when a young animal or a baby is very vulnerable. As a result, there is a high proportion of deaths on the way to maturity. For instance, fish produce enormous numbers of offspring, of which only a few will survive. All the rest die from attacks by predators, shortage of food, the rigours of the environment and so on. Humans have developed, through the course of evolution, the ability of parents to take care of their child, protecting it, feeding it and nurturing it for many years before it 'leaves the nest'.

Another problem of learned behaviour in its broadest sense is that the environment is not always stable: in other words, it changes for one reason or another in the course of time. An example is the fact that bees and ants constantly have to learn the shortest and easiest way to find food. Bees have to relearn each year where the sweetest flowers grow, while ants plod along the best route they can find to a source of seeds or rotting materials. Ants probably follow a leader or foraging 'expert', but how bees communicate with the others in the hive or nest about what direction to fly is still a matter of debate. Humans also have a changing world and the things they must learn are constantly altering due to technological advances. New skills are constantly being required of people as civilization progresses, such as learning how to drive cars as well as to avoid them, and of course adapting to the increasing presence of computers.

Each species has constantly to learn a whole range of behavioural repertoires. This means that there must be some way of forgetting the old ways or routes, which is a form of learning to forget. Ants, bees and cockroaches are capable of learning fairly simple things, and a whole group of neurobiologists devote a great deal of time and ingenuity to ascertaining, under laboratory conditions as well as in the natural habitat, what these insects can learn, how they remember, and how their memory can be either improved or disrupted. Although this may have a connection to human learning, it does not often seem to the innocent or uninformed bystander to be particularly relevant to learning and memory in humans. However, research on insect behaviour has in fact provided much of the evidence for understanding the basics of nerve cell networks. Insects have the advantage of being easy to obtain and breed as well has having no particular lobby determined to protect their 'rights'. Although, strictly speaking, insects do not have a central nervous system, as do fish, birds and mammals, they have a series of clusters of nerve cells, called ganglia, which are a primitive form of brain.

The most popular insects for laboratory studies in recent years for both learning and memory have been fruit flies (*Drosophila melanogaster*). The advantage of these very simple organisms is not only that they can learn and remember different smells and tastes, but that they are capable of being altered by mutating their nervous system with radiation or chemicals. In various laboratories, mutant fruit flies have been produced which can learn but not remember, or which have an instant, almost photographic memory, or which cannot learn at all. The basic chemical steps in the process of learning and the consolidation of memory will be discussed in Chapter 4, where it will be shown that these processes also involve some trigger of the genetic apparatus, the genome, of all living things.

CHAPTER TWO

The brain

'The brain is the most complicated kilo of matter in the universe.'
Anon.

The human brain, as everyone knows, is an organ the size of a small melon located in the head. It is protected by the skull and by a series of membranes, thin sheets of cells between the bone and brain matter, bathed in a liquid called the cerebrospinal fluid (CSF). This colourless liquid, which consists mainly of water with various proteins, salts and small molecules, fills the ventricles, helps transport materials to the brain and removes debris. The inward transport actually begins with cerebral blood flow, which carries oxygen from the lungs and nutrients from the food in the stomach to the brain and spinal cord – the central nervous system. The skull, membranes and CSF also hold the brain matter together and provide some cushioning against sudden jolts.

The brain itself is fairly soft, with the consistency of a soft-boiled egg. Since many people have seen animal brains either frozen in butcher's shops or as anatomical specimens pickled in formaldehyde or preserved in alcohol, there is a general impression that the brain is more solid that it actually is. The brain has a whitish colour, flecked with pink, due to the blood in the small capillaries at its surface. This external surface, as is seen in so many drawings or models, is deeply furrowed and criss-crossed by an intricate pattern of ridges and valleys, giving it the appear-ance of a very large walnut. In monkeys, apes and particularly humans, these convolutions increase the surface of the outer layer of the brain. This is one of the most important 'improvements' in the nervous system brought about by evolution. The brains of mice and rats have a relatively smooth outer surface, while cats and dogs have some indentations. But it is only monkeys, and particularly apes, that have convolutions that are almost as complex as those of humans.

The brain of a rat is about the size of an almond and smooth, and when the cortex, the outer layer, is peeled off by careful dissection and flattened, it has an area about the size of a large postage stamp. On the other hand, when the cortex of the human brain is peeled off and flattened, it covers an area about the size of a page of newsprint. The increase in the area of the cortex or outer layer of the brain has the advantage of increasing the number of cells that can be packed into it, while retaining a sheet-like organization. If the processing of things such as vision or memory occurs in the cortex, as we believe it does, this gives a distinct advantage to any organism with many furrows on the surface of the brain, i.e. a relatively large number of cortical cells. The mechanism for processing activity in the cortex, for dealing with sensory information and memory, will be discussed in the next two chapters.

A great deal has been said about brain size (i.e. weight) and its relationship to mental capacity and intelligence. On comparing various species of mammals, the absolute size of the brain has very little meaning, since an elephant's brain is obviously very much heavier than that of any other mammal. For comparative studies, a more meaningful measure has been used in which brain weight is related to body weight (or, sometimes, to body length from the nose to the tip of the tail). However, there is currently no general agreement about whether relative brain size can be correlated with intelligence or mental ability. The weight of an elephant's brain is only 0.2 per cent of its body weight. It turns out that of all the mammals, the tree shrew, a small mouse-like animal of no great distinction – intellectual or otherwise – has the biggest relative brain size, 3 per cent of body weight. The tree shrew is vaguely related to the elephant, which by tradition is supposed to have a good memory. But here the analogy ends. Why the tree shrew should be blessed with a relatively big brain is not at all clear.

Another animal that is said to have an unusually sophisticated intelligence and memory is the dolphin. This is partly due to the misconception that the dolphin is a fish, and fish are known to have relatively small brains and a simple behavioural repertoire. However, the dolphin is a mammal that breathes air through its lungs. The relative brain size of a dolphin is about the same as that of a dog, some breeds of which are known to be extremely clever. It is therefore not surprising that the dolphin can learn to do tricks and use a very sophisticated sonar-like system for communication. There are even reports of dolphins being used for clandestine underwater activities by the American and the former Soviet navies.

Within species, comparative brain sizes become very complicated, as in the case of dogs, which are bred for characteristics other than intelligence. Dogs bred for speed or for long-haired silkiness seem to lose out in intelligence as measured by their ability to distinguish objects in laboratory conditions. Other breeds of dog have been trained to learn and remember smells, and are used for finding drugs and explosives or identifying a burglar from his lost glove. Laboratory rats have been bred for their ability to learn and remember, producing the 'maze-bright' and 'maze-dull' strains, which have different abilities to learn. However, there are many factors that make it very difficult to compare brain size and relate it to function.

Considerable attention has been paid to the size or relative size of the human brain. The first point of interest is that the ratio of brain weight to body weight is at a maximum at birth and decreases with age, reaching a fairly steady level at puberty. In other words, newborn babies have very large brains, relatively speaking, weighing some 300 grams. This is roughly the size of the brain of an adult male chimpanzee. Children and their brains continue to grow for many years, gradually increasing their ability to learn and remember. There have been suggestions that the growth of the brains of children is not steady, but occurs in spurts, each period of rapid growth being associated with a particularly important developmental or intellectual stage. These stages could be the ability to reason abstractly, to talk, or even to do arithmetic. The idea of spurts of brain growth is still around, but has not attracted much enthusiasm.

The possible difference between the relative size of male and female brains of the same age and accounting for differences in weight has inevitably drawn much attention. So far no great difference has been found in relative size between ethnic groups – a very controversial subject. Obviously the brain of a petite Javanese teenager is very much smaller than that of a giant Russian peasant boy. But when brain size is adjusted for size or weight of the body, there does not appear to be any great advantage for either. Moreover, in measuring intelligence one has, of course, to take into account the effects of education and cultural background.

Individual brain sizes, particularly of famous people, have also attracted attention, but with very few real results. Oliver Cromwell and Karl Gauss (the famous German physicist) are said to have had very large brains, and Voltaire, a particularly small one. Much depends on how brain weight was determined, whether it was weighed under identical conditions or account taken of the loss of blood and other liquids, and how it was preserved. I doubt whether very much can be drawn from these observations. The brain of Albert Einstein, an intellectual giant of the twentieth century, has intrigued many people. It is said to have been relatively large, and parts of it were recently discovered lovingly preserved in formaldehyde, by an admirer, somewhere in the USA. It was suggested that his genius might have been due to the size or number of certain brain cells. However, on careful examination, very little difference was found between the brain cells of Einstein and those of other people.

In summary, the weight of the average adult human brain ranges between about 1000 and 1500 grams. The brains of females, who usually weigh less, are at the lower end of the scale. The brain can, in many ways, be considered the most complicated kilo of matter in the universe. Although overall, the brain has a gelatinous texture, its main feature is that it is not uniform in structure, but consists of many areas that differ in colour, consistency and function, as was noted by Galen 1800 years ago. It is the study of the role of these areas, and their interconnections and relationship to function, that is the main occupation of many neuroscientists.

One of the major problems in studying the brain is its complexity, the great extent of its functions, and its consequent range in space and time. Space or size implies that brain functions (such as vision, sensitivity to drugs and pain, and memory) can be investigated at various levels. Some scientists, molecular neurobiologists, concentrate on the role of molecules in the brain, from the very simplest such as water (the main constituent of CSF), oxygen and cholesterol, to the large molecular chains of proteins, enzymes and DNA, which are thousands of times larger. Other scientists studying the brain – neurobiologists – focus on the neurons (specialized nerve cells, or parts of them – the nucleus, the outer membrane and the connections between them) and other cells in the CNS. Neurons were discovered by chance by an Italian anatomist, Camillo Golgi, who shared the Nobel Prize for this, about a hundred years ago. He was looking at thin slices of brain tissue that were stained with a solution of silver nitrate. It turned out that about 10 per cent of the neurons in each slice were specifically stained black.

Living cells are like tiny islands – self-contained and surrounded by a fatty membrane, rather like a sandy beach with occasional indentations and rocks. Neurons, the basic building blocks of the brain and nervous system, are exceptional. First, they are 'excitable' cells: that is, they transmit electric impulses along the fibres that connect them. These impulses are very fast, reaching over 500 kilometres per hour. This means that, over the very short distances between cells, such impulses take only milliseconds – a few thousandths of a second. The adult brain has about 10 billion neurons packed into it – approximately equal to the number of trees in the Amazon tropical rain forest, or roughly the number of people in the entire world in about twenty years' time.

Each neuron is connected to other excitable cells by means of up to a thousand 'processes' or thin fibres which send and receive information. These processes are of two kinds: dendrites, which are like branched trees that receive nerve impulses, and axons, which are single fibres that transmit information to other neurons. The way this works will be discussed later. Some of these fibres are short, while others are up to a metre long. It has been calculated that, if all the fibres in a single human brain were spun into a single thread, it could be wrapped around the earth forty times.

Until very recently, neurons, unlike most other cells, were considered unable to divide. It was thought that neurons could die, but were never created by cell division in a mature brain. This is, nowadays, not considered to be exactly true, which may provide some hope for those with serious brain damage.

Apart from the millions of neurons in the human brain, there are many other cells, known collectively as glia (from the Greek for glue). There are almost ten times as many glia as there are neurons. They are part of an elaborate support system for the brain, transporting nutrients, removing waste materials, and providing insulation around axons for the bioelectric system. There is currently a new wave of interest in glia, but neurons still have all the publicity.

A large group of neuroscientists are interested in a more complex area, the study of networks of cells – from thousands of cells in the ganglia of invertebrates and insects, to millions of cells linked together in various brain regions of birds and mammals. A very different approach, once entirely separate, is that of studying the whole brain, as psychologists, many physiologists and those interested in behaviour do. This includes the 'simpler' brains of invertebrates, fish and birds, as well as the final challenge: the complex brains of primates and, in particular, of people. The range in size from the study of molecules to that of the whole organ covers, in the language of scientists, about seven orders of magnitude: that is, 10 million fold. This enormous range presents many difficulties not only in the techniques, but also in the concepts to be used. As a result, neurobiologists have tended to concentrate their research on a given range based on 'the size of the problem'.

The brain is divided into many regions, such as the cortex, the hip-pocampus and the amygdala – an almond shaped area concerned with emotion. A vibrant area of activity for neuroanatomists and neuro-physiologists is the connection between these areas and function. There are hundreds of such regions, which can be identified only by specialists. Among those interested in the whole brain are cognitive neuroscientists, who have recently begun to integrate their interests with those of psy-chologists and zoologists – concerned with the behaviour of invert-ebrates, chicks, rats, monkeys and humans. Finally, there is also an increasingly important group of mathematicians and computer-oriented scientists who have joined the great enterprise – research on the brain – and who are concerned with 'models' of the brain. Many of these are involved in the development of a very interesting field, artificial intel-ligence (AI), which involves attempts to develop computer programs capable of performing a whole range of complex mental tasks, including playing world-class chess. AI, in fact, is the basis of most modern robot technology, otherwise known as robotics.

None of these groups of scientists have a monopoly on the understanding of the way the brain works, and their interests often encompass more than one subdivision. But by working together they will, in the not so distant future, reach the ultimate goal – understanding how the brain works, and particularly the riddle of learning and memory. The importance of this enterprise can be judged by the fact that UNESCO designated the 1990s as the decade of the brain. The size and scope of brain research, i.e. neuroscience, is also indicated by the fact that 30,000 participants now attend the major annual conference on the subject, whereas some thirty years ago fewer than 2000 used to meet. Another way of looking at it is to consider the enormous number of topics discussed at neuroscience conferences. These include the development and regeneration of the nervous system, the molecular and cell biology of neurons, glia and their components, the chemicals specific to the brain, the way the senses operate, and various aspects of behaviour, including learning and memory, and the effects of ageing and disease.

Another indication of the specialization in brain study is given by the techniques or apparatus used, and the great range of time scales involved. Time scales can spread over ten orders of magnitude: that is, 10 billion fold. Some experiments are based on measurements of events lasting a few thousandths of a second (milliseconds), during which time very fast electrochemical processes occur. This is the time required for ions, such as potassium or calcium, to move through a membrane or in and out of a nerve cell. It is also the time required for an electrochemical impulse (or action potential) to occur in a nerve cell. Other researchers conduct experiments that last from minutes to the hours which are required for cells to grow. These experiments can extend from hours to days if learning and memory in rats or in people are being considered. Developmental neuroscientists, on the other hand, are interested in processes that last over months and even years – the time it takes for various organisms, from rats to humans, to develop through the numerous stages from a fertilized egg to very old age, and death. Then there are those neuroscientists concerned with the evolution of specific brain regions and functions, such as speech. It took millions of years for humans to develop language as a means of communication, as well as the ability to reason, to solve complex problems, and even to plan ahead.

The neuroscientists of today must, therefore, investigate a range of sizes from molecules to the whole brain, and a range of time scales from milliseconds to hours, days and years. The choice really depends on their training and aptitude, the more so since many of the new techniques require years of study and practice. Since the end of the Second World War, research on the brain has become increasingly popular, so that it is now within the capabilities and expertise of hundreds of laboratories and thousands of research workers throughout the world. For this purpose a whole range of instruments and techniques for studying the brain and its functions has been developed. Most of them are very sophisticated and complicated, and require large sums of money; almost all are computerized in one way or another. There are probably around two dozen important techniques used in brain research today. Some are capable of looking at very rapid events, others at individual molecules and others still at a particular function such as vision or the various types of memory.

The earliest neuroscientists were electrophysiologists, who were concerned with studying the very rapid changes in the nervous system using electrodes and other probes in or near the nerve cells in the brains of rats, cats and monkeys. Even the electrophysiology of the minute 'brains', or ganglia, of cockroaches and flies has been studied. However, a major obstacle for those interested in studying human behaviour were the ethical and practical restrictions on looking inside the brains of living people. The work of Wilder Penfield, who could electrically stimulate the various parts of the brains of patients undergoing surgery for epilepsy, has been mentioned in Chapter 1. Alternatively, various 'safe' or non-invasive techniques, such as EEG (electro-encephalograms) and, very recently, MEG (magneto-encephalograms), can measure changes in electric or magnetic fields inside a living, functioning human brain. EEGs have been very popular for decades in the monitoring of events from outside of the head, by means of very sensitive detectors clamped to the skull, which are capable of obtaining measurements between a millisecond and a second. In research using anaesthetized animals, electrodes can be inserted into the brain through holes in the skull, which can give even more precise information once their exact location is known. In order to reduce damage to the nervous system, these electrodes are very fine and fragile. This research has yielded very important information over the past fifty years, including the understanding of sensory input –

pain, vision, touch, smell, taste and sound (see Chapter 3).

Electrophysiology is also one of the most important techniques used in the study of learning and memory. However, the behavioural range of the simpler animals (flies, sea slugs and so on) is so limited that only the basic neural processes can be studied. In studies involving more developed animals, there has still been the problem of finding convincing 'models' of human problems, such as depression, stress and even the various types of memory (see Chapter 4).

Recently an extraordinary new area of research has been opened up with the development of new, even more powerful non-invasive techniques, which could be used on people without worrying about the ethics or practicalities. Using such techniques, a whole range of behaviours from attention and fear to language, dreaming and the various types of memory could be examined from outside the head. The leading methods are positron emission tomography (PET) and the 'jewel in the crown', functional magnetic resonance imaging (fMRI). Imaging is now the name of the game in brain research, aiming to relate the beautiful coloured maps and pictures made by PET and fMRI machines to events happening in the brain at the cellular and regional levels. One of the most exciting areas in recent years is the increased understanding of the involvement of the human hippocampus and cortex in the processing, storing and retrieval of information, i.e. learning and memory.

For many years the three major approaches to studying the brain were known colloquially as 'sparks', 'soup' and 'plumbing'. 'Sparks' is a term for electrophysiology, i.e. the study of bioelectric currents almost unique to brain cells. EEG and recordings from implanted electrodes are its major techniques. In fact, what is measured is not electricity in the usual sense, which is electron flow conducted by metal wires, but the electric currents caused by very rapid movement of potassium and sodium ions in and out of nerve cells. The imbalance of ions inside and outside is essentially the source of bioelectricity, which can then be picked up by EEGs in humans or implanted electrodes in animals.

'Soup' was an approach that became increasingly fashionable in the middle part of the twentieth century among those with a chemical background – the neurochemists. The name 'soup' came from the basic technique of cutting up parts of the brain and homogenizing them in a kitchen blender or similar apparatus. This formed a kind of soup, which was then analysed for its chemical composition. The brains were usually those of rats, although occasionally larger brains were used, such as sheep or ox brains and even those of humans – post mortem.

The first aim of the neurochemists was to determine the amount of different substances in the brain and their distribution. However, it must be remembered that between 60 and 70 per cent of the brain, as of any living tissue, is water, and that much of the 'action' in the brain takes place in a watery environment. Water has a unique capacity to dissolve salts, and some salts have a vital role in brain function. Potassium salts are needed for the electrical action of brain cells, although potassium is also essential in other parts of the body. Sodium salts are, of course, ubiquitous, and it has been suggested that an excess of sodium may be related to high blood pressure. However, in the brain, sodium derivatives serve as a kind of background to all the chemical activity there. Magnesium salts are also important in the brain and are needed, like iron, for enzyme action. Iron has, of course, another major role as part of haemoglobin, the material in red blood cells that transports oxygen around the body. Calcium salts also have a very specific and increasingly interesting role as triggers of biochemical processes in the brain – a very hot subject for research these days.

One of the first surprises that neurochemists found, in the first half of the twentieth century, was that there are small amounts of substances – the neurotransmitters – which are unique to the brain and are not found in any other part of the body. The neurotransmitters are, in fact, the key to the way nerve cells communicate with one another, across the synaptic gaps. These gaps control the route and speed with which messages are sent around the brain – the 'enchanted loom', as Sherrington called it. He first suggested that the loom is interrupted at key points – at the junctions between neurons – by means of a tiny gap (thousandths of a millimetre wide), across which the nerve impulse can continue only by the movement of neurotransmitters from one side to another. These might be compared to minute ferries which control and restrict brain function. At the right moment, they are released from one side, diffuse across the gap, and activate a receptor (a large protein) on the other side. This is, in fact, the secret of neurotransmission.

A particularly important neurotransmitter for memory is acetylcholine (ACh). Another is dopamine (DA), a key transmitter involved in movement, emotion, attention and therefore cognition; its role in memory is only now beginning to be understood. There are dozens (perhaps over fifty) other neurotransmitters, many in very small amounts, and confined to specific areas of the brain. They include serotonin, a neurotransmitter that seems to be involved in sleep, mood and particularly depression, and many peptides – small chains of amino acids that are very similar to hormones. An example are the enkephalins and endorphins, which are involved in pain and in drug addiction. These peptides account for the close connection between the endocrine (hormonal) and nervous systems.

The number of identified neurotransmitters increases from year to year as the chemical methods of detection become more refined. However, their distribution throughout the brain is very uneven and their specific actions are quite difficult to determine. A great deal of research today is devoted to understanding the action of neurotransmitters and the enzymes that make and destroy them. This research was once conducted only in universities and medical schools, but nowadays it is done in the research labs of pharmacological companies interested in CNS drugs as well. The aim has been the treatment of mental disorders and neurological diseases, and in the last decade, the development of medication for 'improving' memory.

The biggest surprise for neurochemists and neuropharmacologists was the discovery a few years ago that a simple gas, nitric oxide (NO), is a neurotransmitter as well as being a well-known item in the secondary school and university chemistry curriculum. This transmitter, unlike the others, is a gas that dissolves in brain fluids and is apparently involved in brain systems dealing with mood, the action of the heart and impotence. It also has a role in memory, although it is not entirely clear what this role is. Although very impressive results were obtained by the 'soup' approach, the very fact that brain tissue was ground up eliminated one of the most important aspects of the central nervous system – its intimate, detailed structure. The soup approach might be compared to grinding up a delicate watch in a mortar and then using the broken parts to try to understand how it once told the time.

An improvement in the overall 'soup' approach was made when it was found that, instead of using lumps of brain, it is possible to dissect and separate individual nerve cells and even specific parts of nerve cells. Alternatively, neuroscientists are able to grow small slices of brain tissue – mostly taken from rodents – in dishes of nutrients with a supply of oxygen. This technique of 'tissue culture' of specific regions of the brain enabled the effect of drugs and various electrical treatments to be studied under controlled conditions. One of the latter is called long-term potentiation (LTP), a series of high-frequency electrical pulses given to a single neuron or group of neurons. This is a model of learning and memory that has been very much in vogue in recent years. There has been considerable criticism of the interpretation of its results, but the model is still very popular.

'Plumbing' is a somewhat derogatory term for those interested in neuroanatomy – the structure and, to some extent, the function of different brain areas. This includes the route and function of optic nerves, the fibres connecting the retina in the eye to the brain. Other sensory systems link up to different parts of the brain for processing via a succession of relay stations (see Chapter 3). Another popular aspect of the plumbing approach is the study of the spinal cord and the connections from the brain to the rest of the body and the limbs. This has attracted all those interested in movement, such as grasping or walking, as well as those concerned with pain, and the autonomic or visceral action of the body – heartbeat, breathing and digestion.

A great deal of time and effort has been spent in dissecting brains, both human and animal, and finding structures in them that differ in function, colour and consistency. Some of these were named after their discoverers, such as the French neuroanatomist Paul Broca, who found a damaged area in the front left-hand side of the post-mortem brain of one of his patients who could not pronounce words. Similarly, the Austrian neuroanatomist Carl Wernike found, when he examined the brains of patients who could only speak gibberish, that an entirely different area was damaged. It became apparent that there is a very subtle, but crucial division of function among different areas and groups of cells in the brain.

By now, almost a hundred areas of the brain have been given names (usually those of their discoverers) and often been subdivided into numbers. However, for the general reader, the main brain areas of interest are the cortex, the hippocampus and perhaps the cerebellum at the lower part of the back of the head, which is concerned with balance. The cortex – or outer peel – appears to be subdivided into specialized zones. The visual cortex at the upper part of the back of the head deals with vision, while the motor cortex, which controls movement, and the auditory cortex, controlling hearing, are at the sides. These areas are not very clearly delineated in humans, overlapping to some extent with one another. Another area of the cortex, the so-called somatosensory cortex, is highly developed in humans and in those mammals, such as monkeys and apes, with highly sensitive tactile hands and fingers.

However, there is no simple one-to-one correspondence between the senses and specific areas of the brain, although many interesting maps linking various brain functions to structure have been made. Such mapping was once the dream of phrenologists or students of the 'mind', such as the Viennese physician Franz Gall in the nineteenth century, who tried to relate bumps and bulges on the skull, which might reflect distortions in the brain below, with certain human characteristics and abilities. This idea has long since fallen into disfavour and has been forgotten by most neuroscientists.

For many decades, neuroanatomists and neurophysiologists were particularly interested in the blood supply to the brain and made maps of the intricate pathways in which blood is supplied to different regions, known as regional cerebral blood flow (rCBF). This was initially based on very careful dissection of both human and animal brains. Apart from its intrinsic interest, this research was of value in locating the areas where minor strokes or mental infarcts might have occurred. Most of the basic information was obtained by painstaking post-mortem dissection and examination of the detailed structure of brain tissue. The location of tiny blood capillaries in each area was determined by carefully cutting thin sections of brain which had been frozen of 'fixed' (i.e. pickled in formalin), and examining them under a microscope. In this way, an accurate map of the blood vessels in the brains of men and animals was made, but it was almost devoid of any understanding of function.

A great breakthrough was made when, during the Second World War, a method was found in the USA of labelling the blood flowing into the living, human brain. By the subject breathing a harmless, inert gas such as nitrous oxide, for a few minutes, the rate at which this label entered and left the brain could be measured. It should be emphasized that nitrous oxide (N_2O) is inert (although it is sometimes used as an anaesthetic by dentists), whereas nitric oxide (NO), as we have seen, is a very active neurotransmitter in the brain.

Fairly complicated mathematical equations were needed to work out the overall rate of flow, but the detailed distribution of blood in the brain of a living human being could still not be determined. This problem was solved some time later in Denmark by what is now a fairly routine technique. This involves the use of an inert radioactive gas (xenon) as a tracer or label for regional cerebral blood flow measurements. It should be noted that the amount of radioactivity is very small – insufficient to cause any serious damage to the brain. The progress and distribution of this radioactivity can be measured over the course of time or treatment by means of a battery of detectors built into a sort of motor-scooter helmet worn by the subject. In order to convert the measurements of radioactivity into a map of blood flow in specified areas of the brain, computerized techniques are used. As better detectors, faster computers and more sophisticated methods of calculation became available, this became one of the most significant advances in brain research.

A few years ago this technique was further refined by using a radioactive form of oxygen, oxygen-15. This has the advantage of having a short half-life – the radioactivity exists for only a few minutes and then disappears. Again the damage from radiation is minimal. This technique is called positron emission tomography (PET) because it uses radioactive isotopes, called positron emitters, which exist for only a few minutes. Radioactive oxygen-15 is used either in water or as a gas. It has to be made in a cyclotron, a fairly expensive type of 'atom smasher' which must be located very near the subject, so that the labelled air or water can enter his or her blood stream within a minute or so. Specially designed cyclotrons have been made for PET studies which are no larger than a domestic refrigerator and make not only oxygen-15, but also a number of other short-lived positron emitters. The most important of these are fluorine-18 and carbon-11. Fluorine is a very reactive element and therefore easily attached to many key molecules (such as anti-depressants) without affecting their biochemical pathways. The use of these positron emitters has enormously enhanced the possibilities of studying the brain, although they can also be used for research on the heart and kidneys.

The rationale behind using PET is that those areas of the brain that 'work harder', i.e. where neurons are most active, have higher blood flow and metabolism. The PET technique displays cross-sections or artificial slices of the brain (tomograms), so that the areas of higher activity are given a colour – usually red for high activity and blue for low activity. This is an artificial coloration that is made by a computer. The enormous success in the use of PET has been its ability to correlate areas of high metabolic activity with various mental processes, such as word forming, vision, moving various limbs, and the many stages and types of memory.

Carbon-11 can be incorporated on the spot into various important molecules required by the brain, using fairly sophisticated chemistry. An essential carbon-containing material is glucose, the sugar that is the major fuel for the production of energy in the brain. The amount and location of glucose in any area and at a given time, again indicated by 'false' colours, can give a very accurate picture of the activity going on at that site. Each week some new application of PET is reported in the scientific journals, by cognitive psychologists and other neuroscientists trying to understand where and how in the brain such activities as thinking or dreaming occur.

The great interest in studying brain physiology and function in a living human brain without surgery, i.e. using non-invasive methods, has drawn the attention of scientists working in another, apparently unrelated field. This is nuclear magnetic resonance (NMR), a very complicated technique that enables atoms of nearly every element to be detected when placed in a very strong magnetic field. Every atom in a molecule located between the poles of these magnets can be detected and processed by computers to present the data as imaginary brain slices, or tomograms. NMR has rapidly become a leading tool for research in organic chemistry, enabling the detailed structure of molecules to be determined.

Since the discovery of NMR in the 1950s, increasingly powerful and precise magnets have been built specifically for studying various molecules in living people – known as whole-body NMR. In brain studies, NMR was originally used to display the distribution of water in the brain, using very fast computers to present the data, again in the form of coloured tomograms. More sophisticated applications to biology and medicine soon followed, and today a powerful, non-invasive technique known as functional magnetic resonance imaging (fMRI) has become almost routine. The word 'nuclear' was dropped from the original name because of its frightening connotations, particularly during the height of the anti-nuclear demonstrations, in order to reduce the anxiety that might be caused to patients who assumed that it was connected with nuclear power or weapons. Functional MRI also measures regional blood flow based on the differences in the magnetic properties of blood with or without oxygen. In the latest developments, the maps produced by PET and fMRI can be combined so that a very sophisticated analysis of brain structure can be examined and correlated with function. In the future, the combination of fMRI and EEG or MEG is an exciting possibility. It should be remembered that the colours are false and in fact are analogous to medieval maps whose makers decided arbitrarily on specific colours for countries and empires. This makes it easier to interpret at a glance, though it must again be emphasized that the reds, greens, yellows, and blues in both fMRI or PET have no significance whatsoever and must be compared to a scale of colours printed down the side.

Great advances have been made in the construction of magnets that are very stable, but large enough to have room between the poles for the head or whole body of an average-sized human. Some machines have a giant, doughnut-shaped magnet above the head. However, the routine use of fMRI still has some problems. One is positioning the head so that it cannot move during a single study, which, like taking photographs in the past, can last up to twenty minutes. In addition, a great effort has to be made to relocate the head in exactly the same position for repeated brain scans, in order to compare studies of the effect of treatment or of changes in the brain over time.

These new techniques (PET and fMRI), have enabled neuroscientists to match behaviour with the anatomy and what is more exciting, the function of the human brain. In the next decade or so we will be able to analyse, and hopefully understand, the mechanism by which we perceive, learn and remember all that goes on around us. The input from the world enters our brains via the senses. How that is done will be discussed in the following chapter.

CHAPTER THREE

The six senses

'Last scene of all ... is second childishness, and mere oblivion, sans teeth, sans eyes, sans taste, sans everything.'

As You Like It (William Shakespeare, 1564–1616)

The above quotation is part of Jacques' soliloquy in *As You Like It*, describing the ravages of age on the senses. By 'sans everything', Shakespeare was no doubt implying loss of memory, a major characteristic of old age. As will be discussed in Chapter 5, loss of memory is the sum total of a number of steps – the first being difficulties with the input of information via the various sensory systems. The fading with age of the senses and of memory is a well-known fact. The first steps of the various sensory inputs into the brain which lead to the learning of skills and the recording of various types of memory will be described in this chapter.

Most people believe that they see, hear, smell and taste real things in a real world. However, 'things' that are perceived are, in reality, particles, waves or molecules that are interpreted by the sensory nervous system and recorded by the brain. The world outside is converted into electrochemical discharges, and processed and recorded in the central nervous system. It appears that during all waking hours we are constantly sensing the outside world, checking continuously for both internal and external changes. The exceptions are when we are unconscious or in a very deep sleep. Our lives, and those of all living things with a nervous system, depend on our success in sensing the world in which we live, making decisions and adjusting our responses accordingly.

The aim of all living things is survival and reproduction. Very simple single-cell organisms such as amoeba can detect changes in light intensity, heat or the availability of food, and respond by moving either towards food (i.e. glucose) or away from noxious stimuli. Many scientists have tried to 'train' these single cells – to teach them to respond – by changing their behaviour. It was hoped to find evidence that information can somehow be stored in a single cell, but there has been little success. Single-celled algae, such as the coloured scum in stagnant pools and rivers, do indeed have a rhythm, an internal clock that controls energy production, which is triggered by light, or sensitivity to chemical stimulants. Obviously, these unicellular organisms must be able to sense changes in light intensity, temperature or the presence of chemicals, but exactly how this is done is not at all clear. In many cases, oddly enough, this internal clock persists in such cells when the nucleus – the genetic apparatus that is supposed to control everything – has been removed.

As life evolved with the formation of multicellular organisms, a rudimentary sensing or nervous system developed in the form of nerve nets and ganglia – clusters of nerve cells. Its main function was again to provide a better (i.e. quicker, more efficient) system for detecting outside stimuli. A great deal of research has been done on the sensory systems of such organisms, ranging from sea slugs (Aplysia) to octopuses. The advantage of these animals is that they have only between a few thousand and hundreds of thousands of nerve cells devoted to the senses. It was thought that primitive animals such as octopuses that respond to touch might be a good model for the sensory systems in mammals and even in humans. But it turned out to be very complicated because octopuses have eight legs instead of two and, as we shall see, there are now better methods for directly understanding human senses such as touch.

There are six senses in humans – five concerned with monitoring the outside world, and one, more subtle, the sense of equilibrium (sensitivity to gravity, rotation, etc.). Vision, which is based on the retina – layers of special cells lining the inside of the eye – is sensitive to size, colour, contrast, brightness and motion of objects, and accounts for a very large part (up to 70 per cent) of the sensory input in humans. Rats, on the other hand, although tested extensively in mazes, rely to a lesser extent on light as a source of information. Like most nocturnal animals, they have a well-developed sense of smell, where a few molecules wafted into the nostrils signal the presence of food or the difference between a predator and another rat, or even trigger the complex pattern of mating.

Hearing is also highly developed in many animals, based on sensitivity in the ears to air-borne pressure. Such changes in pressure are in some cases water-borne, enabling sounds to be 'heard' by mammals that live in the sea, such as whales and dolphins. In all mammals and birds, an organ, the ear, was developed over the course of evolution in order to detect subtle changes in air pressure and convert them into elec- trochemical signals. Smell and taste (known as the olfactory and gus- tatory systems) probably evolved from the primitive cell surface senses of amoeba and algae. In vertebrates, animals with backbones, sensors to taste are concentrated in the tongue, which can detect minute amounts of sweet, sour, bitter or salty substances. Finally the sense of touch involves complex sensitivity to pressure, temperature, pain and vibration, based on sensors embedded in the skin or hairs protruding from it. The common mechanism of all these is detection of a change in stimuli by an outside sensor, conversion to electrical messages, and transmission along nerves through a series of intermediate relay stations to the brain, where the incoming information is analysed and stored by a process known as memory. The methods of selection, storage and retrieval are an essential component of survival and reproduction.

This chapter will describe some of the essential elements of the human sensory systems, making some comparisons with other animals, and starting with the simplest but least studied senses, taste and smell – the chemosenses. The stimuli in both cases are chemical – single molecules that fit into proteins, known as receptors, in the tongue, the roof of the mouth or the upper reaches of the nose. This is a basic mechanism of locks (receptor proteins) and keys (molecules that trigger cascades of biochemical processes), and is used over and over again in living systems. It is how enzymes work, how antibodies handle noxious bacteria, how the blood rids itself of aged, unviable blood cells, and how nerve cells communicate with one another by means of neurotransmitters. In each case, very large glycoproteins, known as receptors, are embedded in cell membranes. Each has one or more cavities or 'active sites' tailored by trial and error over millions of years of evolution. In this very selective system only one or two out of millions of possible keys can fit each receptor lock.

The difference between taste and smell is that taste deals with water-borne molecules in food and drink, whereas smell is concerned with air-borne chemicals released from rotting vegetation, flowers, perfumes, other people, and so on. In the case of taste, the receptors (or locks) are located in different areas of the tongue – bitter at the back near the throat, sweet at the front, sour and salty at the sides. The receptors are embedded on the surface of the tongue near what are called 'taste buds', each consisting of twenty-five to fifty cells. These bumps on the tongue probably help it to grasp food and may not, as many people think, be directly involved in taste. The action of taste receptors is aided by saliva, a watery solution that coats the tongue, dissolves the bitter, sweet, sour or salty molecules, and distributes them over the tongue and parts of the palate (upper mouth). The perceived taste of any substance seems to be due to the combined firing of a number of receptors. The adult human mouth has some 10,000 taste buds, but as people age they tend to lose them, as will be described later in this chapter.

There is a significant difference in taste preference and sensitivity within and between species. For instance, humans and rats like both sucrose and saccharine, dogs dislike saccharine and cats are indifferent to both. Some fish, such as the catfish, have chemosensors all over their body, effectively making them a 'living tongue'. The common house fly has chemosensors on its feet, which enable it to detect sweet or edible things on touchdown. It is well known that salmon return from the open sea to their home base in certain rivers guided by the taste of the water, i.e. by the complicated mixture of molecules dissolved in it. Like anything based on molecules, there is a minimum number that can activate a biological process such as taste or smell. This is known as the threshold, and it differs markedly from species to species and from individual to individual. There is a strong genetic component to these senses, since some quite healthy people are from birth totally unable to taste or smell certain substances. There is in addition a learned or adapted element, which is still being investigated. In summary, taste involves signals travelling along a chain of neurons from the tongue to the brain, but is affected by appetite and emotion, hence the effect of hunger and mood on taste.

The related sense of smell is also based on molecules, which activate receptors in the nose, triggering a whole chemical and bioelectrical cascade from the nose all the way to the olfactory centres in the brain, where the information is processed and recorded. This is part of the 'primitive' portion of the brain known as the limbic system. Animals are very dependent on an acute sense of smell, which is not as carefully controlled as vision and sound by higher functions of the brain. Most wild animals such as rats and deer, as well as those that have been domesticated, particularly dogs, have low thresholds for smell. In other words, their olfactory sensitivity is very high and few molecules are required to produce a signal.

The mechanism for deciding what action to take following detection of a certain smell is complex and not fully understood. However, many male animals can detect and get aroused by a very few molecules, known as pheromones, released from a potential mate. Insects, incidentally, are particularly sensitive to a few molecules of pheromones released into the air by a female, over a mile away. It is not clear whether male humans can be 'turned on' by a specific female pheromone (or vice versa) and some perfume-making companies have been exploring this possibility. On the whole, the answer seems to be negative. There are still many unexplained problems related to the sense of smell, such as why it is so difficult to describe an odour (unlike a sound or a visual scene) and what role genetics play. In other words, is an acute sense of smell inherited or, as seems to be the case in police sniffer dogs, is it enhanced by training?

The human olfactory system depends on about 10 million cells in the nasal cavities, which relay specific signals to the brain. This sensitivity to smell has spawned a whole industry and even supports some national economies – from the nutmeg and cinnamon plantations of the Spice Islands, and French perfumes, to the entire food and drink industries, as well as the manufacture of cosmetics, soaps and detergents. The commercialization of the sense of smell and its associations in the brain has been carried even further by some supermarkets, which release the 'smell' of freshly baked bread or just-brewed coffee into their food departments through the air-conditioning system. This is supposed to trigger a pleasant association with food and increase the feeling of well-being among the customers, ultimately causing them to spend more money. It is said that, for similar reasons, some flower shops use a chrysanthemum spray to give the impression of freshness.

Everyone knows that police dogs are trained to use their superior sense of smell to identify explosives in suitcases, criminals in line-ups, dangerous drugs in packages, and even bodies in the ruins of bombed buildings. In each case it appears that only a few molecules of some volatile material, emitted from sweat, processed heroin or plastic explosive (Semtex), are sufficient. These special dogs undergo prolonged training by being rewarded with an appropriate titbit following successful performance. This is possible because certain strains of dogs have ten times as many olfactory receptor cells as a human being, and a relatively much larger area of the cerebral cortex for analysing smells. A good sniffer dog can detect an odour 10,000 times weaker than a human being can. Human beings nevertheless have a reasonable sense of smell, using the 10 million olfactory receptor cells in their nasal cavities to enable them to identify thousands of different smells.

It seems that there is a difference between sniffing and smelling. Sniffing causes a rush of air through the nostrils, determined by their size, shape and position, which is needed to activate the olfactory system. A single tongue is apparently sufficient for the sense of taste, whereas, as we shall see, two eyes and two ears are needed to determine the distance and movement of sources of light or sound.

Human hearing is fairly acute, but not as sensitive as that of many animals. Again, trained watchdogs and most animals have a remarkable ability to detect sounds and even changes in tone and pitch. Pitch, tone and volume (loudness) are the parameters of sound – pitch being the number of vibrations per second (measured in units called Hertz), high-frequency sounds being shrill and low frequencies producing deep tones. 'Hearing a sound' is initiated when waves in the air hit thin, flexible, skin-like membranes, the ear drums, each the size of a little fingernail inside the ear. These intermittent pulses are converted via a chain of very small bones, membranes and fluids in the inner ear, into nerve signals that lead to the hearing centres of the brain, the auditory cortex, to be decoded, analysed and compared with similar patterns in the memory store (see memory for music in Chapter 4). Memory for sounds and for identifying music is quite complex, which is why it has not yet been possible to explain how one can tune in and focus on a single instrument in a full orchestra or react to a sudden sound (a shot or breaking glass) by a series of sharp movements – the 'startle' reflex.

Some animals have, through evolution, perfected their ability to detect sounds in the dark – a kind of sonar. Bats, for instance, can emit a very high-pitched squeak (usually inaudible to humans), and detect the sound waves reflected by solid objects such as walls and trees in order to be able to navigate at night. Other examples of species with a specially developed sense of hearing are sea snails, squids and other invertebrates that use sound for communication and navigation in an aquatic environment. Dolphins have a remarkably sensitive sonar system based on a clicking sound for the detection of objects or mates underwater, and the great sperm whale can produce a characteristic 'song', a mixture of clicks, grunts and moans, which other whales can pick up miles away.

A great deal of research is now devoted to identifying exactly what the pathways of the auditory system are in the human brain, using the latest non-invasive techniques, fMRI and PET (see Chapter 2). One interesting area of research is how and why only certain people can be trained to be musicians and opera singers, and others not. There is, apparently, a very intricate memory system for sound in the brain, an interesting example of which is the increased sensitivity of mothers of many animals, and most humans, to detect and identify the cries of distress of their own offspring. In most adults there is also the related ability to learn to hear and attend to sounds selectively – the 'cocktail party' phenomenon. Nevertheless it appears to be very difficult for most people to attend to simultaneous sounds or conversations, particularly as they get older. The strategy usually used is to ignore each one in turn and shift attention back and forth, but how this is done is not known. Most animals, including humans, can determine the source of a sound by measuring the very small differences in time it takes to activate each ear drum. This involves a type of memory known as an echoic memory, which will be discussed in Chapter 4.

The sense of touch in its various forms has been extensively investigated by psychologists and physiologists. There appear to be three types of receptor for touch – those for pressure, those for pain, and those for temperature. As in all sensory systems, the sense of touch is based on receptors sensitive to pressure located near the surface of the skin all over the body. Some of these receptors are close together in places such as the fingertips and the lips, their distribution ranging from a few hundreds to many thousands per square millimetre of skin. These receptors convert pressure on the skin to bioelectricity, which is conducted onward, by nerve fibres packed into the spinal cord, to the body-sensing (somatosensory) area of the cortex for analysis and processing. In addition to touch, some receptors also react to vibration. As with other senses, when vision is dimmed another sense, such as sound or touch, takes over. Examples of this are blind people who have a super sensitivity to sounds, to feel and identify objects, and read braille very rapidly, using their fingertips.

The sense and memory of pain have attracted attention ever since the Greek physician Galen studied wounded gladiators and experimented on piglets 1800 years ago. We now know that the sensation begins with specialized, bush-shaped cells embedded in the skin, known as 'free nerve endings', since they lack the membranes associated with other sensory cells. Pain receptors also exist inside the body, such as those in or near the roots of teeth. The receptors have evolved like those for other chemosensors, to be activated by molecules released by certain types of damage. This can be physical (cuts or abrasions), chemical (acids), thermal (hot kettles) or even microbial. They are distributed unevenly throughout the body, being most abundant in the facial skin, less so at the back of the legs, and entirely absent in the brain. It is an odd fact that once the scalp, skull and associated membranes are removed (under anaesthetic), neurosurgeons can operate on a living brain without causing the patient any pain. The bioelectric signals of pain, like those for touch, travel along nerve fibres up the spinal cord to the brain, the difference being that pain signals can be modified or even blocked by other neurons on the way, whereas touch signals are unaffected.

There is enormous literature (and even an international Pain Society) devoted to the study of different kinds of pain (acute, dull and chronic). There is particular interest in the effect of various drugs, including local anaesthetics and analgesics (aspirin and morphine), pain thresholds and emotions on sensitivity to pain. The interactions between different pathways involved in pain is apparently the basis of acupuncture. A particularly intriguing phenomenon related to memory is 'phantom pain', an often painful sensation that some amputees feel in the tips of their fingers or toes which have been removed by surgery. This sensation is apparently real, very baffling, and related to some kind of memory or record of 'body sense'. This is an active, though rather specialized area of research.

The sense of equilibrium or balance is different from other senses, in that it is really a process in which the brain uses a range of inputs to work out which muscles in the arms and particularly legs must be moved to keep erect. Balance is much in the news these days, since it is related to gravity and of much concern to astronauts and cosmonauts as well as, of course, to acrobats. In humans, equilibrium or balance is detected by a special mechanism in the inner ear that transmits signals to the cerebellum to be processed. This input plus information from the visual system as well as sensors in the soles of the feet provide an unconscious, inner feeling of what is 'upright'. The sense of position or of balance is almost instinctive in most animals. The growth and development of embryos, simple organisms and plants are currently being studied in orbiting space laboratories in order to investigate their reactions to gravity or the lack of it. All fish and some aquatic animals have a separate system for keeping their orientation in the water based on a swim bladder.

An enormous evolutionary step in mammals was the transition from walking on four legs to bipedal locomotion (using two legs) by the common ancestor of humans and apes. The development of two-legged gait evolved over millions of years, due to the advantage in the savannas of Africa of freeing the front legs or paws and having hands for gathering, throwing, holding and manipulating objects. Walking on two legs must be learned by humans, whereas the newborn of many animals, such as calves, foals and even monkeys, can almost instinctively get up and run. Learning to walk is one of the hallmarks of the human species, together with other skills that must be learned and remembered, such as feeding oneself, throwing things and eventually writing, typing, using a computer, playing the guitar or piano, and participating in a vast number of sports. All these are in the domain of motor control, i.e. the brain–muscle connection. There are many stories, which may be apocryphal, about how children who were brought up by monkeys or wolves never learned to walk or talk – Rudyard Kipling's Mowgli, raised by animals in the jungles of India, is probably one of the more famous fictional heroes of this genre.

Vision is without doubt the most elaborate and useful sensory system in humans. It is essential for the survival of almost all animals (except bats and moles) and very highly developed in birds. Eagles, owls and other birds of prey can spot a tiny mouse from a very great height or distance, gauge its speed and direction, and pounce on it, unerringly. To be able to do this, they have evolved a particularly sensitive and very fast visual system for processing information, based on the existence of two eyes and two separate optic nerves leading to the brain. I will not discuss here the complexities of the invertebrate visual system, where different types of light-sensing system, such as those of insects, have evolved.

The mammalian visual system, including that of humans, can be likened to a camera, or rather two parallel cameras, located in the front of the head. Each 'camera' or eye has a lens at the front of the eyeball which can move slightly in its socket in order to focus incoming rays of light. These rays or particles (photons) are reflected from the sun, moon, candle or lamp by objects in the surroundings. The photons enter the eye through a small hole (the pupil) in the front, which is surrounded by the coloured part (the iris), which is instinctively adjusted for the level or amount of illumination. The lens, pupil and iris are further protected by an additional external lens, the cornea. As in old-fashioned cameras, the rays of light of different frequency and intensity are focused by the lens on to an array of light-sensitive cells about the size and thickness of a postage stamp, lining the back of the eyeball. Here the analogy of a camera ends and the visual system becomes more like a TV camera or one of the latest electronic, filmless cameras. In the eye, the image is converted by the retinal cells into bioelectrical impulses, which are conveyed via a number of steps in the optic nerve to the visual cortex at the back of the head. This is a very large area of the brain where an incredible amount of action occurs. During waking hours, each eye sends millions of signals every second, along thousands of fibres, for analysis, interpretation and recording (i.e. perceiving, learning and memory). Various muscles can adjust the size of the pupil, and the position and shape of the lens, in order to focus the image on to the retinal cells, of which there are two types, differing in shape and function. Each human eye contains about 10 million rod-like cells – the rods – which can detect shades of black and white, and about 5 to 7 million cone-like cells – the cones – which detect colours. The structure and chemistry of these cells and the finer points of colour vision and their conversion to bioelectric signals for transmission to the brain will not be discussed here; nor will I elaborate on colour blindness, a genetic defect in a subtype of cones, which afflicts about 10 per cent of the male population, myself included.

The main feature of the human visual system, which involves a large proportion of the cells in the brain, is the conversion from the light falling on rods and cones and its integration and processing by various back-up cells (bipolar, horizontal and so on), and the transmission along the optic nerve to various relay stations and regions in the brain. These regions are given the names V1 to V5, each of which deals with initial sorting, comparison of colours and contrasts, detection of angles, edges and motion, etc. An enormous amount of research and several Nobel prizes have been devoted to the analysis of the visual system in humans as well as in cats and monkeys. Some neuroscientists have concentrated on the electro- or biochemistry of the neurons in the system; others on the interaction between different cell types and nerve pathways, i.e. visual networks.

An interesting area of research is in the development of the visual system: in other words, how cells in the potential retina of the embryo eye (of a frog or a human being) find and connect to the correct areas of the visual cortex in the brain. It seems that the neural fibres grow according to a genetically controlled program, but are also fine-tuned by gradients of some as yet unidentified chemicals in the embryonic brain. Then there is the problem of how the brain of a child (or a tadpole) learns to organize visual information and account for the fact that the image on the retina is upside down, and that during every waking second the distance, relative size, position and direction of movement of objects have to be calculated and recorded. The development of an under-standing of movement, speed and direction was neatly summed up some years ago by Jerry Lettvin of the Massachusetts Institute of Technology, in a wonderful article, 'What the frog's eye tells the frog's brain'.

There are many interesting anomalies in the visual system. First, there is the merging of a rapid succession (up to sixty per second) of images from a moving object which gives the illusion of movement. Then there is the related 'flicker fusion', which accounts for the appearance of smooth movement on cinema screens. Another much studied anomaly is the optical (or, more accurately, visual) illusion, where two networks of neurons compete or give conflicting information.

Dreams can also be considered part of the activities of the visual system. During certain types of sleep, when the eyes are closed and no light can enter, the brain can create its own images and events, which appear almost real. The biochemical mechanism and purpose of dreaming is still not understood, but it appears that it may be due to an essential activity related to biochemical processing, giving the illusion of information coming in from the outside. The interpretation or 'meaning' of dreams has been the central occupation of prophets, mediums and soothsayers since ancient times. Even the Bible is full of stories about dreams, such as Jacob's dream of a ladder of angels or Joseph's interpretation of Pharaoh's dream of fat and thin cows, signifying alternating prosperity and famine. Dreaming is also connected to the emotional systems of the brain, and the ability to remember dreams varies with each person. This has been extensively discussed by Sigmund Freud, in his famous book, *The Interpretation of Dreams*.

Some of the most interesting aspects of the human visual system are the identification, learning and memory of symbols such as letters of the alphabet, and mathematical and musical notation, as well as the specific memory for faces and places. These are largely based on the co-ordination of groups of rods and cones in the retina and chains of networks of neurons by what are called 'the higher cognitive functional levels' of the brain. In humans, thousands of nerve fibres and synapses are required to process and identify a single face, and thousands more associate it with the name, the sound of a voice, and perhaps even the recollection of recent conversations and mutual experiences. The identification of a single face takes up to half a second, which is a long time in terms of the speed at which the various intermediate bioelectrical and biochemical steps are made. There are many situations where the visual system is impaired, from short-sightedness and dizziness, to blackouts and strokes. This is the cause of many neurological diseases. The loss of ability to identify a face (prosopagnosia) is caused by strokes or brain damage in accidents. Its treatment is very difficult, but slow progress is being made as more and more is understood about the human visual system.

Before leaving the subject of vision, one could ask: why do humans, apes, monkeys and all mammals have two eyes rather than one? Part of the answer is that binary or two-eyed vision is required to gauge the distance, depth and speed of objects. Some animals, such as fish and horses, have problems with visual judgements because their eyes are on either side of the head. Determining distance and movement is not instinctive, so many animals including humans must learn and remember these skills. Cats brought up from birth with their eyes covered or in total darkness have great difficulties later in judging speeds and distances. When and how the effects of 'visual deprivation' occurs have been studied extensively, and we now know that humans need a prolonged childhood in order to learn and remember processes such as how to catch a ball or understand that something is behind something else. Once learned, these things have to be remembered.

I have so far described each of the senses in adult humans at their peak. As indicated at the beginning of this chapter, I have gone into details of each sensory system because they represent the first step of the input into the memory mechanism. In some cases, particularly vision, an intricate array of neurons does some very rapid, preliminary processing of incoming visual signals, before sending bioelectrical signals to the brain. Part of this very short-term memory system (sensory visual memory) is located in the retinal and associated back-up cells, and some of it along the optic nerve, somewhere between the eye and the brain. This whole area is part of modern psychophysics and is associated with the most advanced ideas in computer modelling of the visual system.

However, as we well know, nothing lasts for ever, particularly things as complex as vision, hearing, smell, taste, touch and the sense of equilibrium. In order to cope with wear and tear, there are many ingenious biochemical mechanisms throughout the body for surveillance: that is, measuring the loss in efficiency of the various systems and their constant renewal. For instance, old red blood cells that are no longer viable (no longer capable of carrying sufficient oxygen) are constantly being identified and removed automatically. In the brain, the ravages of time are dealt with by a complex 'repair and replace' mechanism – much like the periodic overhauls given by garages to a car. However, as time goes on beyond middle age, more and more problems arise that cannot be overcome, as well as mistakes in the repair system itself.

In vision, on which we depend so much for our survival as well as pleasure, various functions become less efficient or effective with age. For instance, in the eyes of some people as they grow older, the cornea, the extra lens that also protects the eye, becomes less transparent due to certain changes in its constituents. In addition, the cornea begins to flatten which, together with alterations in the focusing of the visual image in the eye, requires the use of glasses – or, in more serious cases, corneal transplants. Changes also occur with time in the flexibility of the little muscles that control the iris (i.e. the pupil size), and in the flexibility of the lens. This explains why with age we need 'more light' to read by. An odd phenomenon is the switch from far- to near-sightedness that occurs at or around the age of seventy, due to changes in the lenses of the eye.

Other problems of the visual system are the gradual increase in the opaqueness of the vitreous humour – the jelly-like liquid in the eyeball – and the decrease in the sensitivity of the neurons in the retina. This not only causes our sight to dim, but also makes it more difficult for the eyes to adapt to flashbulbs or the headlights of oncoming cars at night. The changes in the eye with age also include yellowing of the lens and alterations in the colour-sensitive neurons, the cones, in the retina. Thus many older people become less sensitive to the green-blue-violet range of colours, as has been confirmed by direct measurements in old and young people, and which is illustrated by the finding that older artists use less dark blue and violet in their paintings than younger ones do.

The sense of hearing, as we all know, changes for the worse with age. This can include the relatively rare hearing of voices by older people due to the pressure from bulging blood vessels (aneurysms) in parts of the brain dealing with hearing, which can fortunately be dealt with by medication. However, most older people suffer from gradual loss of hearing due to changes in the ear drums, fluids and sound-sensitive cells in their ears. The problems with one-third of older people are simply due to the build-up of ear wax in the outer ear. In the other two-thirds of the population, all in their sixties, seventies and beyond, changes occur inside the ear – the ear drums become less flexible and sensitive to sound waves, and the mechanism for converting sound (air waves) into vibrations of the liquid inside the ear becomes less effective. These changes, together with the death of the neurons that convert these vibrations into electrochemical signals, are the major cause of hearing impairments. There are, of course, individual variations in the sensitivity to certain frequencies, which can be and usually are corrected by modern, electronic hearing aids.

So far I have dealt with the 'bad news' for older people. The 'good news' is that the senses of taste and smell stay intact much longer than might be expected. We are born with tongues, mouths and throats, literally covered with taste receptors for sweet, salty, sour and bitter things. In other words, babies are genetically programmed to eat nearly anything. However, most of these receptors die off fairly quickly, so that by the age of ten, these senses have stabilized. In adolescence and adulthood, humans lose taste cells very, very slowly, so that about half (i.e. about 5000) still remain on the tongues of very old people. Although the sensory part of taste remains intact, the perception and identification of flavours by the brain fades. Why this is so, no one yet knows, but it is evident that most older people become less and less sensitive to tasty food and good wine. This may be physiological, but also may be due to the general apathy and depression from which many old people suffer.

The description and quantification of smell is still problematic. People can describe a face, a landscape or even a ballet in words or notations, but have difficulty with the classification of tastes and odours. There are also differences between people related to the environment – variations caused by their growing up in chemically polluted areas, near gas works, putrid marshes or in smoke-filled homes. In spite of their inability to describe what it is they smell, older people can distinguish the difference between the smell of mint, coffee or anise just as well as teenagers. However, beyond the age of sixty-five, a noticeable deterioration begins which varies between individuals. At present, not enough is known about the sense of smell, how to measure it accurately, and the role of genetics, to reach any definitive conclusion.

The sense of touch is very dependent on age. It has been shown that babies who are held, fondled or caressed are much less likely to have emotional problems later on. This is obviously part of the genetic program for the survival of the human species. In adulthood, of the three types of touch receptor (pressure, pain and temperature) discussed earlier, the first deteriorates faster. By the early age of fifty, many people begin to have less sensitivity to touch, particularly in their extremities – their fingers and feet. Changes in the sensitivity to pain with age is more complicated and is related to the kind of pain as well as to differences in gender and cultural upbringing. For various reasons, some people can tolerate pain well, while others can block out the feelings altogether. In spite of a great interest in this subject, due to the fact that so many older people have problems with wear and tear in their joints, broken bones and various painful diseases, no one quite understands the effects of age and much work remains to be done. Sensitivity to temperature is even more complicated, since the cells or mechanism involved in detecting changes in heat and cold are not fully understood, and nor are the effects of age. In summary, it appears that alterations in neural conduction, in perception, even imagination, and the suddenness of the change, all contribute to the difficulties of sensing temperature by elderly people.

Finally, the sixth sense, equilibrium, is in one way or another closely connected with the others (particularly the inner ear, the eye and the soles of the feet), and also deteriorates with age. This is manifest in the increase in the number of falls in older people, resulting in multiple bruises and broken bones – a very painful problem, for which at present there is no easy remedy.

The next chapter will be devoted to the main topic of this book – memory in its various forms. In the subsequent chapters, the various reasons for the loss and 'regaining' of memory will be discussed. It must be remembered that the memory system consists of a number of parallel and interacting networks. For example, there are apparently different pathways and strategies for remembering faces or painful experiences. Interference, or loss of memory, can occur at any point in these multiple processes, each of which is a chain of steps. It has been difficult to investigate the effect of interventions on some of the very fast sensory processes – the first few milliseconds of input. However, each day new discoveries and technical advances are being made, and I have no doubt that this will be understood during the next decade.

CHAPTER FOUR

Memory and memories

'[Memory] is like a funnel, a sponge, a strainer, and a sieve.'
The Mishnah (2nd to 3rd century, AD)

The word 'memory' is an umbrella term for many things, ranging from memories of childhood and 'autobiographical' memory to the flood of facts recalled from nowhere, perhaps triggered by a television programme. It includes the fascinating problem of memory for faces, which seem to divide into those faces that are easily recalled, such as those of relatives, close friends, film stars and politicians, and other faces that require concentration. Memory also includes learning to recognize and use tools and equipment, often called 'training'. This type of memory is usually more robust and less susceptible to disruption, as has been found in a number of people with specific injuries to a certain area of the brain. These classic medical cases, usually identified only by their initials, are the basis of much that neuroanatomists in the early part of the twentieth century learned about different types of memory and their connection to the structure of the brain.

The memories of taste and smell, as well as sounds, shapes and the feel of things, are directly related to the senses discussed in Chapter 3. They are very often triggered in unexpected ways by cues of which we are not often aware. These include very personal memories like those related to the smell of home cooking, and very general ones such as the warning produced by the smell of unlit gas. Proust's great work, *The Remembrance of Things Past*, starts off with the memory of madeleines, those special French cakes, which trigger off a flood of nostalgia.

It is almost a truism to say that the world today has increasingly become concerned with numbers. Modern life requires one to remember telephone and fax numbers, car registration and identity card numbers, security door lock and bank teller PINs, and so forth. This subject has therefore become an intense area for research. Finally, there is language, one of the great feats of learning and memory in humans, which apparently distinguishes them from all other animals.

Psychologists and neurophysiologists have tried to put order and logic into the understanding of many different types of memory, some of which are highly specific and others rather esoteric. The scientific method for studying any aspect of human life is to use groups of people to control all non-essential variables, such as education and upbringing. This is not easy, even if one wishes to compare identical twins brought up in exactly the same way. This is one reason why animals, and rats in particular, have been so popular among experimental psychologists and those neuroscientists interested in learning and memory. Rats can be inbred for many generations – mating brothers and sisters so that many genetically controlled variables are as similar as possible. This means that their size (i.e. weight) at a particular age, and their response to pain, light, food, hunger, thirst, etc., are the same. It was assumed that inbred animals kept in similar cages in matching rooms would be almost identical, so that their behaviour, and in particular the process of learning and memory when tested in mazes and other devices, would also be very similar. In most laboratories that study rat behaviour, only male animals are used in order to cut down the variability in behaviour caused by the ovarian cycle and other hormonal effects that occur in females. Over the past seventy years, in hundreds of laboratories of experimental psychology and neuropharmacology in drug companies, millions of rats have been used to study activity, resistance to pain, sleep, as well as learning and behaviour in mazes and other devices.

Due to the emergence of non-invasive imaging techniques such as PET and fMRI, described in Chapter 2, more and more research on memory is being done on people rather than rats, particularly the more subtle and, to my mind, the more interesting forms of memory. Here again the method includes trying to control all non-essential variables, which is not easy to do even if the subjects used for experiments are identical twins. In human memory studies, it was important to control the diet, mood and motivation of each individual, whether a child, a student or a memory-impaired adult. Alternatively, the same person could be used as his or her own control, which means being tested under different conditions. In any case, meaningful results are most often obtained using statistics. An exception to this is the work of Hermann Ebbinghaus, who, as will shortly be discussed, did his classical work on memory using only himself as a subject. Students in psychology departments, who are about as uniform a population as might be found – usually between eighteen and twenty-five years old, with much the same background, education, environment and habits – are popular subjects for experiments. They are also easily available, so that a great deal of research on memory has been done in psychology departments, where the participation of students in learning and memory experiments is compulsory.

During the first few decades of the twentieth century, it was established that there are two basic types of memory. The first is short-term memory (STM), also known as 'working' or 'immediate' memory, which is not very robust and can be retrieved a few seconds or, at best, a few minutes later. The second is long-term memory (LTM), which can last from a few minutes to decades, and very often 'for life'. LTM has been gradually divided into various subtypes, which will be discussed later in this chapter.

Short-term (immediate or operational) memory is dependent on attention – very little is remembered if there are any serious distractions. In a typical experiment, if the subjects are instructed to concentrate on a given task, much less is remembered if there is a loud noise or any other distractions in the background. These days much of the information needed for a normal life is visual – maps, phone numbers in directories, post codes, train timetables, and so on. Some of this is transformed in the brain into an acoustic code – a sort of silent echo that appears to make it easier to remember. For this reason, many people repeat names or numbers on first hearing, which helps in remembering them later on.

The best examples of short-term memory and its limitations are related to telephone numbers. When a phone number is given by someone verbally, and there is no way of writing it down, it is often difficult to remember. You can remember the number by repeating it to yourself over and over. But if your attention is distracted by someone talking to you, you will forget the number or get it wrong. Then there is the well-known example of looking up a phone number in a telephone book and dialling it immediately. If the number is engaged or otherwise unobtainable, it is immediately forgotten and has to be looked up again. This is another example of how outside interference and lack of concentration cause difficulties.

A particularly interesting aspect of short-term or operational memory is that it seems to be limited in range or extent: that is, there is a limit to the number of items that can be learned at one time. The number appears to be between five and nine. This is known by psychologists as the 'seven plus or minus two' phenomenon or 'the magic number seven'. However, the number can be increased by grouping some items into larger but manageable units, in a process known as 'chunking'. For example, the very familiar dates of 1492 or 1066 can be treated as a single unit rather than as four digits. Chunking is also the rationale behind the division of long telephone numbers into groups of two, three or four digits. Postcodes in the UK are deliberately made easier to remember by using two- or three-letter and digit halves, such as YO3 7EA. Science educators have recommended using 'chunking' as a means of remembering particularly difficult subjects like chemistry, since by grouping rather boring information into groups of seven items it becomes easier to remember.

As its name implies, short-term memory has a definite time scale – the time it takes to encode incoming information, usually only a few tenths of a second, if numbers or letters are involved. Memory for faces is more complicated, as will be shown later. The importance of short-term memory is that it is an essential step towards permanent storage of information. It follows input from the senses, discussed in Chapter 3, and is disrupted not only by distraction, but also by shock or trauma. It has been known for a long time that people in traffic accidents cannot remember what occurred immediately after – and, what is more interesting, immediately before – an accident. It appears that there is something vulnerable, perhaps a biochemical process, involved in short-term or working memory, which is still not completely understood. Another well-known effect is due to electroconvulsive treatment (ECT) – deliberately giving an electric shock to the brains of rats or seriously depressed patients. This high-voltage shock usually alleviates the condition of depressed people who do not respond to antidepressants, but it can also affect their memory. The adverse effect has in recent years been minimized by confining the electric shock to one side of the brain only and using tranquillizers.

The very first step in transmitting information from the outside world to the brain is sensory memory. This system has evolved in all living creatures, including humans, to sort out information coming in from the senses. Examples in the visual system are the ability to see movement in films, although film is actually the projection of a series of single frames rapidly following one another. Similarly, a lighted cigarette or a glowing ember can be used to 'write' letters or circles in the dark, the motion of a single point of light being seen as a complete line or a circle. It appears that there are at least two components of visual sensory memory. One is located in or very near the retina of the eye, and is strongly influenced by the brightness of the stimulus – the spot of light or picture. The other form of visual or sensory memory appears to be located somewhere along the pathway between the eye and the brain, and is involved mainly in shape recognition.

Similarly, the auditory system also has a brief sensory memory, used to locate the source of a sound. When a sound, say a click or the tone of a bell, arrives in one ear, it is retained until it reaches the other ear. This enables the brain to work out where the source is, and depends on having two ears a number of centimetres apart. As the system involves hearing a sound twice, it is called echoic memory, and it is determined genetically but refined by learning. The analogous word for locating objects in the visual sensory memory is iconic, although its use is less popular.

An interesting subdivision of memory is photographic memory, which is almost instantaneous and very robust. Most, but not all, children have a very good rapid memory for pictures, scenes or the printed page. The technical terms for this is 'eidetic memory'. It is rare in adults because it tends to disappear during adolescence. A photographic memory in some university students may actually indicate a slower rate of development, since they still use childish methods of remembering.

A recent PET study has shown that autobiographical memory is processed in the right side of the brain. Much has been written about differences in neural activity in the right and left hemispheres. On closer analysis, it appears that most activities involve both sides, although one side or other may be predominantly involved in certain steps in the memory chain. Of course, the memory among both children and adults of complex things, such as the sight of a bustling city street, is made easier by linking it to other modalities, such as smell, taste or touch, each one reinforcing the other. This technique is used almost instinctively by Alzheimer's disease patients when their memory begins to fade.

At the beginning of the twentieth century, the German psychologist Hermann Ebbinghaus became the first person to study memory in detail, by carefully planned experiments. In fact, he was the first investigator to break away from a 2000-year tradition and actually do experiments rather than study memory theoretically. Studying only one subject – himself – in the course of a very few years Ebbinghaus produced a reasonably logical theory using experiments in which he tried to learn by recitation strings of nonsense syllables – three-letter combinations that could be pronounced, but had absolutely no meaning at all, such as CAZ, ZOL, WUX and VER. After several hours or days, he tested his memory for these 'words', and examined the effect of the rate at which he memorized them and of various methods of distracting or confusing himself. He even examined the effects of sleep on his ability to recall. His use of nonsense syllables was supposed to remove any bias that might be caused by using real three-letter words. Ebbinghaus was mainly interested in assessing rates of input and retrieval of information, and investigating the reasons for forgetting the 'words'.

The memory for lists of words, as well as languages, requires attention and practice. These are skills that can be learned. The ability of student waiters and waitresses in a restaurant to learn and remember accurately the orders of diners seated at a table was examined. It was found that up to twenty orders could be remembered accurately by experienced waiters. Young waiters soon learned to identify who ordered what by their position around a table. This is much the same way that the Greek mnemonist Simonides remembered the names of people around a table 2000 years ago, as will be discussed later. Many waiters apparently use mental codes for remembering details of different courses, such as using the first letter of each type of food. These techniques make the life of waiters easier and the customers better satisfied. But the memory of restaurant orders does not last long, since the information is apparently stored in a medium-term type of memory, and needs constant rehearsal if it is not to be forgotten.

Neuroscientists, and particularly cognitive psychologists, have been trying to understand the more permanent forms of memory for many years. Many ingenious and elaborate experiments were devised to find out how, when, and even why and where, information is stored in the human brain. Recent research ranges from the very simple example of learning to avoid pain, to remembering the information necessary for people to cope with life – that is, with the environment and, of course, with one another. It soon became clear that different types of information, depending on the content and the senses involved, are dealt with in different ways, follow different rules and, to a large extent, can be considered separate systems.

The most basic memory system is considered by many to be procedural memory, which, as its name implies, deals with activities related to performance. Examples of this type of memory include how to walk – something that every child has to learn and remember. Many animals can solve this problem of co-ordination and balance almost instinctively from birth, largely using the cerebellum, a small, compact appendage to the brain at the back of the head, above the spinal cord. Other examples or procedural memory are how to ride a bicycle and how to drive a car.

As many people know from personal experience, walking, riding a bicycle and driving a car do not need one to be consciously aware of the detailed sequence of steps; all that is needed is to begin with a few seconds or minutes of concentration or attention. A particular feature of procedural memory is that it is hard to articulate – that is, to express or explain in simple words – and that the information lasts a very long time, as those who are confronted with bicycles in adulthood can attest. Procedural memory is resistant to change and, once set, is very difficult to modify or rearrange. This can be seen from the problems people have when changing from a stick shift to an automatic gear.

A great deal of research has been done on the effect of brain damage on procedural memory. It appears that certain amnesic patients, who have difficulty in remembering what they have just been told, have little trouble in remembering skills learned long ago, and no problem in learning new skills. This is probably due to the fact that these patients do not have to know much about the context – that is, the circumstances under which they learned this skill – but merely need to remember the routine. This seems to indicate that procedural memory is a separate system following its own rules.

A higher-level system is called semantic memory, which is concerned with general knowledge about the world at large. It does not concern any specific events in an individual's life or experience, and might be called an encyclopaedia of facts about the world. Semantic memory is acquired by observation and by learning, and, like procedural memory, is retained intact for a long time. A marked difference is that semantic memory can be articulated in words – in fact, as its name implies, it is mainly concerned with words and is related to language and linguistics. It has been studied very intensively in many countries, since it is the very basis of human knowledge and activities. The kinds of facts stored in this memory are the colours of roses, the capital cities of certain countries, the number of centimetres in a metre, and the meaning of words. Most people have a vocabulary of between 20,000 and 50,000 words – some double this – the meanings of which are stored in semantic memory. In addition, there is a vast encyclopaedia of other types of information and is obviously the focus of one of the world's major human activities – education.

Understanding semantic memory is one of the most popular problems in modern philosophy, as well as in the design of advanced computers used for storing data. A great deal of attention has been paid to exactly how such a vast amount of information can be stored in the brain. One suggestion is that it is based on associations or relatedness – information located in the brain is retrieved faster if it is preceded by information (colour, smell, texture) that has similar content. It seems that semantic memory has an ordered structure, and when an item of information of a particular kind is called for, say the capital of a certain country or an historical event, associated concepts are immediately brought to mind, such as a map or a page in a history book. Some psychologists use a special term – schema – to explain how people organize new information, and how they reconstruct things that they may appear to have forgotten. These schemas may be based on visual features, as in recognizing a face or a place, or related to time, as in recalling a sequence of events. Another way of organizing semantic information may be through mental categories, such as objects, events or names.

Perhaps the most interesting type or level of memory is episodic memory. This, like semantic memory, is easily articulated, i.e. it can be described in words, but its content is concerned with events from a person's own life rather than being just general knowledge. Episodic memories are usually related to a specific place and time, and often include a representation of oneself as a participant or an observer. Episodic memory (unlike procedural or semantic memory) is more sensitive to the passage of time, and unless periodically recalled or rehearsed, the main features, if not the event itself, become increasingly blurred. Another feature of episodic memory is that the retrieval of one particular incident is unlikely to be influenced by other, even related, episodes.

A major part of episodic memory is called, for obvious reasons, autobiographical memory, which is stored in a time sequence. Personal recollections or reminiscences can be retrieved as a single incident or a series of events after a period of years. However, they are easier to remember if they are related to a major event in a person's life – starting university, loss of a job, birth of a child, and so on. The retrieval of episodic memory, which includes autobiography, is also sensitive to very dramatic 'landmark' events, such as Kennedy's assassination or the landing on the moon. Extreme examples of this type are often called 'flash bulb' memories. The shock of some dramatic event seems to enhance recall of trivial incidents that occurred simultaneously – where one was at the time, who one was with, and even what they were wearing.

One explanation for this highly detailed information is that such traumatic memories are retrieved, discussed and thought about over and over again. This constant rehearsal may make information easier to retrieve; however, on examination, much of the information is not accurate. This has become a serious legal problem in court, where the consequences of eye-witness testimony can be far more serious than those of personal reminiscences. The problem of 'false memories' is very much in the news these days, as memories of unpleasant incidents in one's childhood (such as physical or sexual abuse) are often extracted by suggestion from psychotherapists and social workers. However, many of the incidents appear to be imaginary, and the guilt and embarrassment of all those concerned is a serious social problem.

Memory for music is a special example of long-term auditory memory. Most ordinary people can remember some tunes, although this ability is somewhat reduced when the music is played by a different instrument or sung by a different voice or in a different key. Expert musicians – both amateurs and professionals – seem to have a prodigious memory for melodies and scores. In Europe, the practice of playing concert music from memory is a relatively recent development. It was only during the second half of the nineteenth century that Franz Lizst and Clara Schumann created a sensation by playing without a score. Today the ability to play from memory is the norm in competitions and concerts. The demands on memory during a single solo piano performance are remarkable, requiring the production of over 1000 notes a minute for up to an hour. In addition to the auditory aspect, memory for music requires a great deal of 'assistance' from motor or tactile memory. It is well known that sitting down at the keyboard or picking up a musical instrument helps to 'clue in' the performer.

There are many stories and studies of individual musicians – performers, composers and conductors – with unusually comprehensive memories. Mozart's talent for remembering scores heard only once is often quoted. He is reported to have heard a performance of *Allegris Misereri* sung by the Vatican choir in Rome, where nobody, on pain of excommunication, was allowed to write down the music. However, after one hearing, he was able to return home and write down the whole piece from memory with almost no mistakes. Incidentally, he is reported to have checked his memory by returning to hear the choir for a second time, and made the few necessary corrections by surreptitiously writing on his hat.

The conductor Toscanini is said to have known by heart every note played by every instrument of some 250 symphonies, and the words and music of about 100 operas, in addition to chamber music, pieces for cello, violin and piano, songs, etc. It is said that just before the NBC orchestra was about to perform a concert, the second bassoonist told the conductor, Toscanini, that the lowest note on his instrument was broken. After only a moment's reflection, Toscanini is said to have replied, 'It's all right, that note doesn't occur in tonight's concert.' There are many such stories about Toscanini and other conductors who have the ability to hear a whole composition in their 'mind's eye'.

The processing and memory for music seems to be mainly, but not entirely, located in the left side of the brain. There is some evidence that professional musicians have an enlarged area on that side which is involved in music. It may also be involved in the sensitivity of about one in 10,000 people to absolute pitch, which occurs from a very early age. The French composer Maurice Ravel suffered severe damage to his left hemisphere in a car accident at the age of fifty-seven, and although he could still hear and appreciate music, he was never again able to play the piano, sing in tune or compose.

Music is a complex mixture of melody, pitch, timbre, harmony and rhythm, combined in an enormous number of ways. The memory of each of these components is probably stored in a different group of brain cells, so that the ability to conduct or compose music – from Bach to rock-and-roll – can be affected in different ways. A neurological disorder – an amnesia for music – usually occurs in musicians who suffer from stroke or other brain damage on the right side. There is also evidence that hearing music activates the electrical activity on the right side of the brain of newborn infants, which seems to be confirmed by more recent studies on adults using PET and fMRI. In summary, memory for music is a very special and interesting talent that involves many regions of the brain, even the cerebellum, and is probably unique to the human species. Attempts are now being made to understand the phenomenon of learning to sight-read music. It would also be interesting to understand the causes of pleasure and emotion elicited by music, opera and ballet.

Cognitive psychologists and other neuroscientists have designated many subdivisions or modalities in addition to those described above, such as declarative memory – information that can be described in words – and non-declarative memory, which is performance based, such as habits. Another division is into verbal memory – for words, names, etc. – and non-verbal memory, which includes remembering journeys, music and faces. Memory has also been subdivided into unique memory, which belongs to one class, such as familiar faces and names, and non-unique memory, which consists of general information about animals, fruit, tools, etc. Then there is explicit memory, which is concerned with what has happened and is processed by the hippocampus, and implicit memory, which deals with how events have occurred. Finally, there is emotional memory, a very popular subject these days, in which the nervous system and the endocrine (hormonal) system seem to be connected. These subdivisions depend, to a large extent, on the methods of testing and the philosophy of the research scientist. With the rapid increase in the use of fMRI and other techniques for correlating various categories of memory with specific areas of the brain, many of these modalities and areas of overlap will disappear.

Before explaining the actual mechanism for analysing, storing and retrieving memory, let us address several important questions. First, is there any limit to the amount of information we can absorb and store? Secondly, how much of the total capacity of the brain is actually used? Many attempts have been made to answer these questions, but the task turns out not to be straightforward. From personal observations and various laboratory tests, there seems to be no limit to the amount of information that an adult human being can absorb and store, although there are, of course, problems due to attention reduction, fatigue and the effects of mood and stress. Many brain functions, such as reaction time, slow down with age, which might appear to limit the capacity of the brain. Two further questions can then be asked: Is there any evidence for differences in the limits of brain capacity which depend on the type or modality of memory? And finally, how much time is required for new information to be received, characterized, routed and stored before even newer information can be dealt with?

There are, at present, no simple or generally accepted answers to any of these questions. Some forty years ago, the theoretical mathematician John von Neuman of the Massachusetts Institute of Technology (one of the founding fathers of computers) tried to calculate the theoretical limit to the amount of information that a single waking adult can take in over a lifetime. He based his calculation on the number of neurons in the brain, and he assumed that each nerve cell can process about fourteen bits of information per second. His estimate for the number of nerve cells in the brain was wrong, and his assumption of the life expectancy of the average human was at that time only sixty years. Using more up-to-date figures, the input over a lifetime comes to an enormous and totally unrealistic number. Alternatively, neuroscientists have tried to estimate the amount of information that the optic nerve carries in the course of a lifetime, since vision accounts for 50–80 per cent of the information entering the human brain. Again these very large numbers tend to meaningless, suggesting that this is the wrong approach to calculating the capacity of the human brain.

A more reasonable calculation is based on the amount of information that can be accumulated by reading, assuming that an average person reads one 'bit' of information per second. This means that a lifetime of reading could result in about 10,000 million items – another enormous number. A different approach is to divide long-term memory into various modalities and subgroups as discussed above, and make a reasonable estimate of the amount of information an average adult can possibly process and store. Verbal information is one of the major inputs into memory and the number of words in most modern languages ranges from 25,000 to 50,000. In fact, most adults get by with only a few thousand words, not counting technical terms. Teenagers know and can remember about half of these, and even six-year-old English speakers can use up to about 10,000 words. This is about two-thirds of all the words used by Shakespeare, who was self-educated and, indeed, rather repetitive. It is interesting to note that, when people are asked the total number of words they know, they grossly underestimate the figure.

A fascinating example of a prodigious visual memory is the perhaps apocryphal story of the Greek poet Simonides of Ceos, who lived during the first century BC. According to the Roman politician and writer Cicero, a Greek nobleman called Scopas gave a banquet in his house to celebrate his victory in wrestling at the Olympic Games. Simonides, a professional orator, was invited to the banquet in order to recite poems in honour of the host. In his recitation he included praise of the twin gods Castor and Pollux, which annoyed Scopas, who told Simonides that he would pay only half of the agreed upon fee, saying that the latter could claim the other half from the gods. Some time later, during the banquet, Simonides was informed that two young men were waiting outside the house to see him. As he went out to meet them, the whole banqueting hall collapsed (presumably due to an earthquake), killing all the guests. The bodies inside the ruins were so mutilated that their relatives could not identify them for burial. However, Simonides, who had escaped this disaster unscathed (unlike the unfortunate Scopas), was able to identify each of the victims by remembering exactly where he or she sat. Cicero hints that the two men outside were the twin gods Castor and Pollux, who rewarded Simonides by saving his life. The point of the story is that Simonides used a method of recalling people and faces by remembering the place where each guest sat. He was therefore able to identify and name each of the bodies, and his name became closely connected with mnemonics, the technique or science of remembering.

Other prodigious feats of memory have been recorded, such as that of Cicero himself, who was said to be able to speak in the Senate for days on end without using notes. Another example is Publius Scipio, a Roman general who was said to be able to remember the names and identify each of the 35,000 men in his army. Simonides' technique of remembering names (or words) by using places in a certain location – either an imaginary theatre or, as in the story, a banqueting hall – led to the use of positions in a 'theatre of the mind' to aid memory. This trick has been used by actors and others concerned with memory for words ever since. Recently various memory competitions and even world championships have been held where, for instance, the time taken to memorize a full pack of randomly ordered playing cards was measured. Some people have trained themselves to remember train timetables, others have specialized in remembering the achievements of all the athletes in each of the Olympic Games, and yet others have memorized the date and day of the week of any event in the past.

Memory for faces is an important feature of human life and society, since a human face can help identify an individual's gender, age and race, and how they feel. It is not clear whether animals recognize or remember faces, since smell has such a major role in their lives. There is an apocryphal story of a chimpanzee who was taught to sort photographs of faces into two piles – one of people and the other of monkeys and apes. He is said to have put pictures of his own face in the 'people' pile. Generally, however, it seems that very few animals recognize faces.

Most people, on the other hand, remember up to a thousand faces fairly easily and can recall some of their names. This number falls off with advancing age, due partly to the sheer number of faces encountered and partly to the other reasons for loss of memory (see chapter 5). With an effort, people can learn to remember about two-thirds of 10,000 different photographs of faces. This should be compared to human language, where up to 100,000 words can be remembered. Things are made easier by the fact that there are fifty basic types of face, which is the core of police identification of criminals: about 50 per cent of all convictions in court are based on line-ups or eye-witness testimony based on remembering a face.

Some people are better at recognizing faces than others, and are also better at identifying paintings and attributing them to the correct painter. This probably indicates a greater attention to detail, but there seems to be no correlation between people's estimate of their ability to recognize the face and how good they really are. Moreover, no correlation has been found between good and poor face recognizers and their ability to remember words. All this supports the idea that there are a number of parallel systems in the brain for dealing with different types of memory. Not surprisingly, memory is much better for familiar faces of friends and celebrities than for unfamiliar faces, and is naturally reduced by tiredness or stress.

Identifying faces usually involves attaching a name to the face, the faces being easier to remember than the names. In tests of long-term memory for faces, it turns out that people remember 70 per cent of the faces they have seen over the past fifty years, but can identify only 20 per cent of the names.

The recall of names is linked to the verbal memory system. But the memory for faces, in monkeys as well as people, is based on specialized 'face' cells. These are apparently sensitive to the characteristic features of a face – and provide information about gender, age, health, mood, attentiveness, and most importantly, intention. This information together with eye contact, facial expression and gestures, is crucial to social interaction. PET studies have shown that the recognition of faces occurs separately from the interpretation of the information conveyed from the face. The right side of the human brain seems to specialize in whole face processing, whereas the left side is concerned with examining the details of various features.

Leonardo da Vinci discussed memory for faces in his book on painting, advising artists to divide a face into four parts – forehead, nose, mouth, and chin – to enable them to remember their sitters or models at a single glance. Surprisingly, he did not mention the eyes. More recently, cognitive psychologists have examined in detail the process of face recognition, which is a skill that starts at a very early age. Babies at birth can see only fuzzy images, but their vision rapidly develops and they soon prefer to look at a picture of a face rather than an abstract scene. The first sight most babies have is usually of people, and they soon learn to interpret expressions and moods. The visual system requires up to 0.5 seconds to identify and remember a face – a relatively long time, which indicates how complex the process is.

Originally, research on face recognition was largely based on the reports of neurologists about people with various brain injuries, whose problems ranged from serious loss of vision to being unable to identify close relatives or recognize themselves in the mirror. Memory for faces is found to be more accurate than for objects such as houses, vehicles and animals. In addition to sensitivity to attractiveness and 'character' in the face it is aided by other cues, such as clothing or voice. It is disproportionately difficult to recognize upside-down faces or negatives of photographs. In the past five years, the understanding of the mechanism and strategy for face recognition has been much improved by using PET and regional cerebral blood flow. The strategy used for identifying faces has been adapted to computers and will soon be used as part of the security system at entrances to buildings, in banks and in airports.

An interesting aspect of the memory of most ordinary people is auto-biographical memory, where out of many thousands of events and details during one's lifetime, some hundreds can be remembered. Of course, musicians, artists and those concerned with special senses, such as wine-tasters and perfume experts, have expanded memories of sounds, tastes and smells. But these do not seem to contribute more than a few thousand items to the repertoire. All in all, one might hazard a guess that the average brain can handle some hundreds of thousands of items of infor-mation under normal circumstances, although, as we have seen, pro-fessional mnemonists are said to be able to remember several hundred thousand facts. Additionally, some people are capable of remembering certain things, usually numbers or words, but are seriously impaired in other ways. The reason for this developmental problem is not yet fully understood.

Originally, the study of learning and attempts to improve memory was confined to particular people – orators and actors. As interest grew in education, attention was focused on the learning process in school children and apprentices. At the same time, a parallel skill evolved bearing little or no relationship to schooling or scholarship – the training of domestic animals, such as hawks, dogs and horses, for hunting or protection. The first dogs were domesticated and trained some 7000 years ago, using the simple rules of reward and punishment. Eventually, domesticated dogs were bred by selection for various qualities, including tracking and guarding, and horses for appearance, warfare and speed. Since Roman times, animals such as bears, lions, elephants and monkeys have been trained for circuses, again by reward and reinforcement. More recently, the training of sea lions, whales and dolphins for 'sea worlds' or 'dolphinariums' has become a major industry.

The earliest research on memory *per se* is much indebted to circuses, where changes or improvements were based on observing behaviour. This approach, called 'behaviourism', became recognized when the Russian physiologist, Pavlov trained dogs to associate the sound of a bell with food. He used an elaborate system for measuring the amount the saliva generated in the stomach, as an indication of response. Although Pavlov's dogs and related experiments by his colleagues are of little direct interest today, they drew considerable attention in the 1920s to the possible use of animals for the systematic study of behaviour in general, and memory in particular.

In order to try and understand the detailed mechanism of recording and retrieving information in the brain, attempts have been made to simplify things by using invertebrates – animals without backbones. As we saw in Chapter 2, fruit flies (*Drosophila melanogaster*) and their various mutants, as well as octopuses and sea slugs (*Aplysia*), have a nervous system based on nerve fibres connected by a nerve net. Instead of brains they have clusters of cells, known as ganglia, that co-ordinate their movement and responses. Invertebrates have the advantage of relatively few nerve cells, only a few tens of thousands, many of which can be identified and labelled with a simple letter and number code, such as A7 or C13.

Unfortunately, invertebrates have a very limited behavioural repertoire, and only very few of the changes become more of less permanent, i.e. serve as a model of long-term memory, so that they have provided only very basic information on the complexities of the mammalian central nervous system. However, the electrochemistry of nervous transmission (based on the movement of sodium and potassium ions) and the chemical reactions involved in neurotransmission across synapses are very similar in the ganglion of a fruit fly or an octopus and the brain of a human being. Some of the same chemicals, including the fifty or so neurotransmitters, are used in different combinations in various parts of the nervous system. A few rare neurotransmitters are unique to lobsters, crabs and other crustaceans, but the principles are the same.

The serious and scientific study of learning and memory under controlled laboratory conditions in birds and mammals is a fairly recent development, starting with rodents and Lashley's fruitless search for the 'engram' or location of memory in the brain. After the Second World War, learning in pigeons became popular due to the fact that they are very intelligent (not at all 'bird-brained'), have excellent eyesight and good memories, and are easy to breed and to train. The intellectual abilities of pigeons had been considered during the war as a method of guiding ballistic missiles to their targets in Japan, by pecking on levers on the side of their cage in the nose cone. This idea led to the well-known 'Skinner box', where pigeons can learn to peck levers in response to a pattern of lights. Harvard psychologist B. F. Skinner later adapted his 'boxes' to the study of learning and memory in rats. Their responses could be automatically and reliably recorded, which made the box simpler and less tedious than using mazes. Skinner boxes were later adapted to the study of learning and memory in monkeys, apes and even children. Chicks have also been a popular animal for memory research, since they can rapidly learn and remember to avoid an unpleasant taste and their brains are sufficiently large and developed to analyse their cellular structure and biochemistry.

The use of an animal model for learning and memory assumes that it is very similar to the human situation. The drawback is, of course, that animals do not talk and cannot be interrogated or tested easily. In fact, language is one of the great differences between people and animals – even the most developed ones, such as apes. The memory for words, i.e. a structured language in humans, is believed to have evolved as a means of communication during hunting, fishing and gathering food. Specific areas of the human brain, dormant in other mammals, were developed for language and have recently been identified by fMRI.

Many attempts have been made to find evidence that chimpanzees, orang-utans and gorillas are capable of using words (nouns, verbs and even adjectives) for communicating with humans. In fact they can, after prolonged training, use tokens representing such words as 'banana', 'red' and 'eat'. In the last forty years or so, computer-based communication was attempted with both monkeys and apes, but although the initial results seemed promising, the experiments turned out to be very difficult to interpret.

Two other major differences between animals and people in relation to brain development are tool using, i.e. the construction and use of objects, and the intriguing but esoteric problem of the concept of 'self', i.e. the realization that 'one' is different from 'the others'. Both of these involve the evolution over hundreds of thousands of years of new pathways and areas in the brain. The definition of tool using or tool making is not a simple matter. In principle, a spider's web and a beaver's dam might be called tools. Animals in the wild are genetically pro-grammed to use techniques for survival that are augmented by obser-vation and by trial and error. However, they do not use insight or appear to make any plans for the future.

Other forms of intelligent behaviour include the dropping by certain birds of a stone on to another species' eggs in order to crack them open and eat the contents, and the use of a stone by sea otters in northern California to crack open molluscs balanced on their chests. The best-known example of tool making is the use by chimpanzees of thin bran-ches deliberately stripped of their leaves in order to prise out termites and other insects from their nests. In the 1920s Wolfgang Kohler showed that chimpanzees can use sticks or a pile of boxes to reach a bunch of bananas suspended from the roof of their cage. Whether this is a case of intuition, learning by observation of the success of other animals or the result of many trials and errors is still not known. Obviously, once successful, the task or behaviour of using a tool becomes easier to remember.

The more elaborate and sophisticated problem of 'self', or in particular 'self-recognition', is more subtle and involves the memory for faces. Human babies apparently learn to recognize themselves in a mirror – or in a similarly shining, reflective, surface – and know that it is 'them' and no other by the age of two or three. Whether or how an animal (a cat, dog, fish or monkey) can, like humans, be taught to identify itself is still an open question. In spite of many efforts in the laboratory, monkeys have been shown to be unable to recognize themselves in the mirror, although some can learn to use mirrors for looking around corners. All other animals, including dogs and cats, have not so far shown any sign of self-recognition in a mirror. Male Siamese fighting fish, who respond aggressively to other males, will attack their own reflection in a mirror placed at the end of their tank until they tire at the lack of response. This is believed to indicate that fish cannot recognize themselves.

A great deal of attention has been paid to the strategies used by children of different ages to learn and remember various tasks, concepts and even languages. Adults have to struggle to learn a new language, whereas small children can pick up a second language apparently with little difficulty. This seems to indicate that young brains have a sort of 'sponge for knowledge', primed to soak up skills and information, which is later lost. Young brains seem to have 'sensitive' periods when connections are made more rapidly between neurons.

After many false starts and diversions, the actual mechanisms of the various types of memory outlined earlier in this chapter are now beginning to make sense. The very rapid events that occur in the eye and ear, known as visual or auditory sensory memory (see Chapter 3), occur in the course of thousandths of a second. Even the transmission of information from the eyes, ears and other senses to the brain is very fast and requires extremely sensitive, special techniques to study it. Until recently, electrophysiology – the 'sparks' approach mentioned in Chapter 2 – was the only method. The next step, the transition from STM to long-term memory – the permanent store – is perhaps the most interesting now that it can be unravelled by fMRI and PET. Karl Lashley showed, over fifty years ago, that there is no single location of memory in the brain, and that the information is distributed over networks and areas (visual, auditory, motor, etc.) throughout the brain. This might be called the 'plumbing approach' in an updated form. Again using fMRI or PET, the connections between clusters of nerve cells (ensembles, as they are sometimes called) are being elucidated. The aim of this work is to determine what is connected to what, and in what sequence the information is recorded, evaluated and retrieved. Unfortunately, even the most modern techniques do not yet have the resolution, i.e. are not sensitive enough, to look at the activity of individual neurons or even very small groups of cells.

The work using implanted electrodes, the size of a human hair, whose position in the brain can be determined very accurately, was of course done on animals. The real challenge for many years has been to sort out the biochemical processes taking place inside neurons and, in particular, in or near synapses. The first attempts by neurochemists to determine what happens at the synapse and how the transition from STM to LTM occurs have been fraught with difficulties. The aim has been to find a link with the overall strategy for memory, first suggested in a fairly simplified form by Donald Hebb. The original Hebbian theory was that certain pathways in the brain are selectively facilitated by simultaneous 'firing' of two or more adjacent synapses. The more modern idea might be called a synthesis of the 'sparks' and updated 'soup' approaches.

Some time ago it was established by classic, rather crude biochemical methods, using invertebrates or thin slices of brain kept alive in a dish, that the 'consolidation' of memory, i.e. the transition from STM to LTM, could be blocked by various chemicals, many of which prevent the synthesis of key proteins. These experiments could be extended to rats, chicks and even aplysia and drosophila, where behaviour could be correlated with the chemical manipulation of neural transmission. Many very subtle experiments have shown that the processes of learning and memory may involve not simple proteins, but rather glycoproteins and glucocorticoids. These are specific proteins or steroid hormones to which various sugars such as glucose are attached. Known as cell-adhesion molecules (CAMs), they are necessary but not sufficient for memory fixation or consolidation. The biochemistry is very complicated and consists of long cascades or chains of events that are gradually being sorted out.

The most important development was the realization that the overall control of neurobiological processes is determined by the DNA in the genes. Not all of these processes are 'expressed' i.e. active but apparently switched on or modified by what are known as 'transcription factors'. The genes are part of the chromosomes inherited by every living being from its parents. This may in some way explain the complicated relationship between nature (i.e. genetics) and nurture (i.e learning). It was found that nerve impulses can activate one or more genes, by a complex chain (or cascade) of molecules and ions, including a number of enzymes, phosphate and calcium ions, and at least one 'transcription factor' – called CREB. These biochemical processes apparently modify the messenger RNA. The changes are made permanent by synthesizing specific proteins, which strengthen existing synapses, thereby facilitating or priming certain neural pathways which can elicit various types of behaviour. The details of the mechanism of these biochemical reactions are still being worked out using all the various invertebrate and animal models. However, it seems likely that, in the course of the next few years, we will at last know in more detail how information coming in from the senses is converted into a permanent store of memory.

Finally, two unusual types of memory must be mentioned. One is the well-known phenomenon of *déjà vu*, in which an unidentified cue triggers off the feeling that something has been seen or heard, or has happened, before. There is as yet no really convincing explanation for this. The second are the so-called collective memories suggested by anthropologists and cultural historians to cover the experience, traditions, ambitions and prejudices of various national or ethnic groups. It is hoped that within the next two or three decades new ideas will be developed to understand these phenomena, as well as ways to complete the missing links in the chain of events leading to memory.

CHAPTER FIVE

Losing one's memory

'Memory is the thing you forget with.'
Alexander Chase, *Perspectives*, 1966

We have seen that neither learning nor memory is easy to define – or to study. Nevertheless, as we enter the twenty-first century, these fundamental processes are beginning, at last, to be understood. We have also seen that with the advent of new techniques (PET and fMRI), and an increasing interaction between neurobiologists, cognitive psychologists and computer specialists, new and exciting advances are to be expected. Together with intensive studies of memory, there is increasing interest in the reverse process – forgetting or loss of memory. A number of issues arise. First, there is a great difference between retrieval and recall. Recall is remembering things or words seen or learned earlier, whereas retrieval is a more general term for extracting things from memory. Both mean forming the right associations and state of mind in order to extract the required information (the number, the name, the date, the face or the fact) from some sort of store. But it is obvious that forgetting or loss of memory is not equal for all systems – semantic, episodic, autobiographical, etc. From personal experience as well as experiments in the lab, it appears that some things are forgotten more rapidly than others. This is similar to the fact that some things are learned more easily than others. Then there is the question: can one deliberately forget?

Before discussing the details of memory loss, a subject that concerns everyone, including those caring for ageing parents or friends, we shall discuss two important questions. First, why remember everything? Secondly, how does 'the brain' decide what to remember? As was discussed in Chapter 4, the limit to the amount of information that a single person can remember is not yet known. However, with some ingenuity and expertise, it has been possible to ascertain how and what animals forget, which is a useful model for loss of memory or forgetting in humans.

The first question – why remember everything? – is quite complicated. It would be useful, from an evolutionary point of view, to remember everything, just in case it might be useful later on. This could include, for instance, remembering the appearance, smell or taste of all poisonous foods. This ability would incidentally have a useful and profound effect on the habits of birds and animals. For instance, a type of memory in animals in the wild, sometimes called 'bait shyness', involves the avoidance of foods that cause sickness or distress. This applies even to very desirable foods and is an important feature of survival. But how can the 'bait' be identified – is it by appearance, smell or even the first taste?

In addition to taste and smell, other senses have a similar impact – the pain from a single electric shock from the grid-floor of a cage is remembered by rats for a very long time. This technique is used extensively in experiments known as 'shock avoidance' for the study of the stages in memory formation, and also for testing the potential usefulness of memory-enhancing drugs. It is also used by many pharmaceutical companies for testing analgesics or pain-killers – CNS drugs that can attenuate or reduce the feeling of pain. Shock avoidance in rats has an analogy in humans. An obvious example of pain avoidance is the apparent life-long fear of hot stoves, radiators and boiling kettles, acquired by most people in childhood, usually by bitter experience. This is, of course, reinforced by vehement warnings expressed by parents. And finally, the memory and avoidance of pain can extend to various phobias, the most common case perhaps being the fear of dentists.

Although it may seem advantageous to remember everything, the concern has been expressed that the brain might become overloaded with information. This is dramatically brought out in the short story of *Funes the Memorious*, by the Argentinian writer, Louis Borges. The story concerns a simple peasant in Argentina who falls from a horse on to his head. As a result, he is able to learn and remember nearly everything, including mathematics, languages and philosophy. Eventually, the strain of so much information becomes too great for him to bear and he dies under tragic circumstances.

The question of whether there is a limit to the 'capacity' of the brain to store information cannot, at present, be answered simply. It certainly looks as if the limit has not been reached, although there does *appear* to be a limit at certain times – caused by fatigue. In simple terms, this means running out of energy or chemicals required to process the storage and retrieval of information. Additionally, boredom can restrict the amount of learning – and, consequently, of memory – through loss of attention or motivation. This is what many school teachers experience, particularly when teaching classes of uninspired pupils. Boredom may eventually cause sleepiness, further contributing to loss of attention. On the other hand a night's sleep is essential to the well-being of all humans (and most animals) in order to provide time for replenishing materials in the brain, removing chemical debris, and perhaps sorting out and storing newly acquired information.

It seems that, if one were to design a memory system that requires a certain time to record, process and perhaps react, it would be best to accept all new information instantaneously without wasting time deciding whether or not it is important. One could then decide later, based on various criteria, what to record. This would enable a small animal, say, to run away from a lion almost immediately it is recognized as such, and not wait to consider which might be the best policy for survival among various alternatives.

In humans, the development of a memory system seems to start almost at the moment of birth. It is not easy to design meaningful experiments that are both reasonable and ethical for newborn babies (neonates). Nevertheless, attempts have been made to measure in the laboratory the responses of babies a few days old to shapes, such as female breasts, faces and sounds. Attempts have also been made to determine how they react to sights, sounds, smells and touch, what is remembered, and for how long. Unlike all lower species, a great deal of the behavioural repertoire of babies is *learned* and not instinctive. Most animals and birds can walk or fly, and react to their surroundings, almost at birth, whereas humans require time, experience and guidance from their parents or minders for many months or even years in order to develop the skills needed to survive. Unlike animals, much of whose behaviour is based on reflexes and coded in the DNA in their genes, very little is instinctive in humans apart from certain reflexes and the autonomous system – breathing, heartbeat and digestion. The head-turning responses of neonates have recently been studied, as well as the basic suckling response, which is a reflex programmed by the genes.

A striking example of the innate behaviour of simple organisms is the web-building ability of the spider, which builds an almost perfect design, with slight adaptations, each time. However, when the web is damaged or partially destroyed, a spider does not know and can never learn how to repair it. It can only start all over again to construct a new web, as perfect as the first one. Humans, on the other hand, learn relatively quickly, from experience or observation, and go on learning all their lives. This is one of the advantages of there being so many nerve cells and pathways in a human brain.

A curious phenomenon that has so far not been explained adequately is known as infantile or childhood amnesia. This is the term used for an age barrier to retrieving childhood memories. Many facts and incidents can be remembered from early childhood, but nothing, apparently, from earlier than about the age of two. Some people claim that they can remember things at an even earlier age, but on careful investigation their memory turns out to be either imagination or, more likely, based on stories or anecdotes told later by parents, grandparents or older siblings.

The most likely explanation of infantile amnesia is that the whole network or 'web' of connections between nerve cells is created in its final form only during the first year or so of life. During this period new connections are made, and the processes between cells are gradually covered with an insulating (myelin) fatty sheath. Surprisingly, the brain is fine-tuned by the death or disappearance of many nerve cells and connections that exist at birth according to a given genetically inherited program. The scientific term for cell death of any kind, now known to be an important feature of development, is apoptosis. It is hard to believe, but nevertheless true, that one is actually born with a relatively complex brain that is gradually simplified by pruning.

Another explanation for infantile amnesia is of a more Freudian character. The first year or two of life is traumatic, involving a noisy, constantly changing and apparently illogical environment in which babies are bombarded by a whole host of largely unpleasant stimuli, to say nothing of being constantly wet or hungry. Memories of this period, like memories of other traumas later in life, are therefore 'repressed'. Whatever the cause, this is an interesting and curious aspect of the early childhood development of the brain.

The standard definition of forgetting is to lose the ability to recall or retrieve facts (or knowledge) – in other words, to be unable to remember, either intentionally or unintentionally. Other, more subtle meanings include neglecting to do something, or being unaware of something or somebody at a particular moment. This introduces the important element of time – the time in which an event occurred and the time at which one wishes or has reason to remember that event. Now that people live longer, this is becoming an increasingly problematic situation, since in the not too distant future 100 years may elapse between the event and the need to remember.

As we get older, most of us will suffer from what used to be called 'benign forgetting'. This form of memory loss, which affects over 95 per cent of the population, has been defined and to some extent clarified by calling it age-associated memory impairment (AAMI), also known as age-associated cognitive impairment (AACI). The definition of this condition in the latest edition of the American Psychiatric Association's catalogue of all defects and diseases related to mental function (known as DSM-IV) has helped to make memory loss in the elderly into a respectable and accepted disorder, so that research can now be supported which will eventually lead to the development of medications and treatments.

Sadly, an increasing proportion of any population suffers from an as yet untreatable problem known as Alzheimer's disease (AD). Some years ago the more cautious term 'senile dementia of the Alzheimer's type' (SDAT) was in fashion, but as the methods of diagnosis improved, the simpler term AD came into general use. In its early stages, this is a very difficult disease to diagnose; its cause is unknown and it is almost impossible to prevent further deterioration. The term AD actually encompasses a number of related forms of the disease, all associated with a rapidly decreasing ability to remember things, particularly those recently learned, heard or seen. The consequent mixture of anger, fear and panic makes life for AD sufferers, and later for their friends and family, increasingly difficult. Fortunately, if one can say so, people with Alzheimer's do not usually live very long – usually a matter of a few years.

The statistics of people suffering from Alzheimer's disease rise from about 3 per cent in the whole population to about double that for those in their sixties. Above this age the numbers increase rapidly, to about 25 or 30 per cent of people in their late eighties. This is a very disquieting figure as an ever-increasing proportion of the population, particularly in the western world, approach this age. This is due, of course, to the fact that the chances of dying from other fatal diseases is constantly decreasing as medical treatment for influenza, hypertension and even cancer improves.

Alzheimer's disease was first described by Alois Alzheimer in 1907. He correlated the cognitive dysfunctions, i.e. loss of memory, in a single female patient, with tiny abnormalities found on her post-mortem brain, when examined under a microscope. He was the first to associate the so-called amyloid *plaques* in certain key areas of her brain with loss of memory and a change in personality. Similar plaques, which are deposits of an unusual protein known as amyloid beta-protein are found in the brains of most people over 85, but they are significantly more numerous in AD patients. This is only one of quite a number of unusual proteins found in their brains. Another significant feature found in brains of AD patients are *tangles*, which are twisted threads of protein associated with apoptosis or neuronal death.

There have been many attempts to find the exact sequence of events that cause AD, but the final answer is not yet known. There is apparently a genetic link to chromosome 21 – a part of the genetic apparatus linked to another distressing neurological disease, Down's syndrome. There are also possible links to other chromosomes, which make understanding the genetic aspects of AD very complex. In a few families in one or two parts of the world, the incidence of the disease – the probability of suffering from it – is inexplicably very high. This may be due to inter-marriage or some, as yet undiscovered, factors. There may even be a separate genetic form of AD, sometimes known as familial Alzheimer's. All the various forms of AD are characterized by a decline not only in recent or working memory, but in cognitive functions in general, and patients suffer from what in medical terms is called dementia.

Except in rare cases, onset occurs in late middle age and progression and degeneration are relatively rapid. In younger patients, the term pre-senile dementia was once used, but is no longer in fashion. There have been reports that the incidence of AD is higher in women than in men, but this may be due merely to the fact that women generally live longer than men. It has also been reported that there is some difference between the incidence in Europe and that in the USA. This is again due to difficulties in diagnosis and to 'fashion'. AD is more talked about in the USA, whereas in Europe the emphasis is on loss of memory in general, including problems with cerebral blood supply caused by mini-strokes in the brain, known as multi-infarct dementia (MID). This is very different from and much rarer than Alzheimer's, but its outward signs can cause confusion between the two. AD is said to be rare among certain groups of people – the Cree Indians of North America, and in Nigeria. If these observations are true, no satisfactory explanation has so far been presented.

Apart from the complex genetic link, various other risk factors have been suggested, including previous head injuries, hypo-thyroidism, various venereal diseases and, curiously, a low level of education. A better education may protect people against AD, perhaps by building up a cognitive reserve: in other words, increasing the network of nerve cell connections early in life may delay the effects of the disease later on. One could say that a PhD may, indeed, prevent AD.

The difficulties in diagnosing AD, and distinguishing it from normal memory lapses, are due in part to its insidious nature. In the early stages, the typical signs are fairly commonplace and easy to confuse with normal ageing. They include absent-mindedness, a tendency to fatigue, difficulty in recalling familiar words and recognizing faces, and an inability to learn new things. Two tell-tale signs are more significant, which are usually apparent to relatives and friends, if not to the patients themselves. These are a deterioration in judgement and social behaviour, and an impatience or restlessness often leading to aggressiveness – obviously due to frustration. As the disease progresses, patients find it increasingly difficult to focus on more than one external stimulus at a time, such as conversations involving several people. AD patients soon develop various defensive mechanisms, such as taking long pauses before replying to a question, or giving rapid, over-confident answers.

In advanced AD, cognitive and other difficulties increase so that loss of memory is commonplace, the ability to follow simple instructions is lost, and the irritability and frustration turn into abusiveness, and even physical aggression. The lack of recognition of familiar faces, particularly of relatives and friends, becomes increasingly distressing. As well as suffering a decline in intellectual capacity, AD patients become increasingly helpless and cannot live or survive alone. Since no cure has yet become available, a number or organizations and societies have been established for mutual support and the exchange of information.

Various tests for AD have been suggested based on the performance of the patients themselves, such as the mini-mental state exam (MMSE), or on the opinions of relatives, friends and carers. Many attempts have been made to improve early diagnosis, which until now has been based largely on a process of elimination. There are indications that PET or fMRI might be useful for detecting AD early on, and the possibility is being explored that the analysis of blood samples for a tell-tale protein may be useful.

A rather surprising set of subjects for the study of memory loss are members of the Roman Catholic School of Sisters of Notre Dame in Mankato, Minnesota in the USA. These nuns make ideal subjects because they all have a similar lifestyle, which almost eliminates variations in environmental factors, such as diet and daily routine. Owing to their sheltered lives, these nuns live to an average age of eighty-five, many living into their nineties and a few reaching 100. However, they lead an active intellectual life, solving crosswords and other puzzles, and participating in word games and contests of memory. Apart from volunteering for studies on ageing and brain function, these nuns have kept detailed journals for most of their lives and have agreed to allow post-mortem studies of the detailed structure and chemistry of their brains as well as an examination of their diaries.

Correlations have been made between the cognitive abilities of the nuns at relatively advanced ages and the prevalence and distribution of plaques and tangles found after death in their brains. In addition, a suggestion has been made that the style of their autobiographical journals might be useful for diagnosis. Those who kept diaries with a reliance on names, dates and facts were found to be more likely to develop AD than those with a rich style full of imagination, ornamentation and ideas. The idea is that the tendency to AD started to appear in early life, long before it became apparent in cognitive tests, so that those nuns liable to get Alzheimer's had to rely heavily on facts rather than on imagination. This might be due to a higher number of connections between brain cells, or higher amounts of essential chemicals in the nervous system in those who are less likely to get AD. These ideas have not yet been accepted by the scientific community. However, the Roman Catholic sisters are an unusual example of the attempts to find uniform groups of very old people for the detailed study of their brains and memory.

Besides the complex genetic link mentioned above, various causes have been suggested for the onset of AD. As with many other diseases, it was once proposed that a virus or even a simple but virulent retrovirus (like HIV, which is implicated in AIDS, a disease where dementia is involved in the later stages) could be the cause. However, no evidence has so far been found to substantiate this theory.

There has also been persistent interest and concern about the connection between the very common metal aluminium and Alzheimer's disease. Aluminium is fairly widely distributed in the earth's crust as a component of many rocks and minerals. It is, in fact, the third most abundant element (after oxygen and silicon) on the surface of the earth. For many years it has been extracted, refined and used extensively in its metallic form in aircraft construction, for wrapping foodstuffs, in the manufacture of kitchen utensils, and increasingly as a lightweight component of furniture and cars. Aluminium salts were also used in certain medications, such as anti-perspirants and antacid tablets, in order to reduce local acidity either in perspiration or the stomach. As a result of fears that there may be some connection to AD, most of these medications now contain magnesium instead of aluminium.

The relationship between aluminium and AD has been very tenuous. It started with the observation that when very large doses of aluminium salts were given to experimental animals, either by injection or in the food, some kind of amnesia (loss of memory) was caused and their brains appeared to contain defects not unlike the classic plaques and tangles.

Similar effects on brain cells were found when brain tissue was grown in culture (in plastic dishes with nutrients), and treated with aluminium salts. However, it must be emphasized that these effects require far larger doses than those likely to be encountered by ordinary people. Such experiments are also not easily reproduced.

Other evidence on aluminium is even less convincing. There have been persistent reports that minute traces of aluminium were found in the brains (even in the plaques and tangles) of people who died after suffering advanced forms of AD. If this is indeed true, an alternative suggestion is that these aluminium-containing deposits may be the result and not the cause of AD. In fact, the plaques and tangles of aberrant protein may 'scavenge' (i.e. extract from the blood stream) tiny traces of aluminium introduced through the diet from the environment. There were also reports that the incidence of AD was more prevalent in certain areas of the USA where aluminium was naturally abundant in the drinking water. These results were subsequently found to be unreliable. All in all, the aluminium theory of AD is currently in disfavour and there does not seem to be much solid evidence for it. Like many other popular views or worries about toxic materials in the food, there is a 'waxing and waning fashion' and aluminium toxicity is definitely out of fashion. This means that there is at present no reason for discarding cooking pots and pans made of aluminium.

The real tragedy for Alzheimer's patients and their families is that there is no clear-cut treatment for the disease even in the early stages. The current recommended treatment is Tacrine, alone or in combination with other drugs. This somewhat poisonous substance is known to block a key enzyme in the turnover of acetylcholine, a neurotransmitter implicated in the processing of memory.

Finally, in the wake of efforts (with mixed success) to use brain transplants for the treatment of Parkinson's disease in humans, the attempt has been made in some laboratories, at least in animal models of Alzheimer's, to replace the affected areas with new brain cells. In Parkinson's the problem was simpler, since the defect, or lesion, is located in a relatively small area about the size of a pea. However, the death of brain cells in AD occurs in many areas of the brain. In addition to the problem of finding a good model of AD in animals (usually rats), there are formidable technical difficulties in replacing dead or dying neurons. As in Parkinsonism, there is still some uncertainty regarding the source of the new cells for transplantation – should they be taken from embryos, cadavers or brain cells grown in culture? It also turns out that other factors, or growth-promoting substances, must be added to the transplanted tissue, and no one yet knows exactly where or how the transplants must be placed – next to or merely near the site of the dead or dying cells. A whole range of moral and ethical questions arise from cerebral cell transplants, such as whether they may cause changes in personality and whether it is reasonable even to try such a complex and expensive procedure on very old people. Famous people who had or are suffering from AD have helped draw attention to the tragedy of the disease, ranging from the writer Jonathan Swift and the actress Rita Hayworth, to Ronald Reagan, the former President of the United States.

Although most people do not have Alzheimer's, many suffer increasingly from loss of memory. There are problems with measuring this loss, with the tests used for determining the effects of age on cognitive ability in ordinary people. For instance, most intelligence tests tend to depend on both knowledge and speed of reaction to questions or questionnaires. A sixty-year-old person usually possesses at least three times the vocabulary and four times the amount of information that a twenty-year-old does. However, the speed of processing in the visual and auditory sensory systems and the rate of conduction of information to the brain are reduced in older people. This may give the impression that their intelligence is lower. However, standard IQ tests take into account the problem of comparison and suggest that intelligence is not affected by age.

Most forms of memory are easier to measure, although the problem of comparison remains. Is an individual's ability to remember, recall or retrieve information to be compared to what similarly aged people remember, or to what that individual's ability was when he or she was much younger? For instance, in testing the memory for a list of 24 words, after a certain time twenty-year-olds remember 14 items from the list, forty-year-olds remember 11 on average, sixty-year-olds remember 8 or 9, and eighty-year-olds barely 6 words. The problem here is of recall, which requires an active memory search and retrieval. Recognition is much easier and much less affected by age.

Special tests are now used for all measurements of memory, such as the Wexler Memory Scale (WMS) or the more general test of intellectual ability, the Wexler Adult Intelligence Scale (WAIS). Each of these written tests is subdivided into various categories, such as vocabulary, digit span and picture recognition. There are various ways of analysing the subdivisions of memory, one of which is simply to determine which things are forgotten. A recent study showed that 83 per cent of elderly people forget names, about 60 per cent lose keys, and about 50 per cent cannot remember what was just said. Going down the list, it turns out that only 40 per cent forget faces or directions, and even fewer forget what they have just done, such as lock the door.

A number of factors could cause the loss of memory in normal adults. As explained earlier, the brain as a whole requires an enormous amount of energy, which is produced by the combustion (burning) of organic material, mostly sugars and other carbohydrates inside each one of the billions of different brain cells. It has been calculated that the total amount of energy required by the awake brain at any one time, is enough to light up a 70W bulb, which can illuminate a very large room. Although the brain of a normal adult weights only about 2 per cent of the total body weight, some 20 per cent of the oxygen breathed in through the lungs is diverted to the brain. This ten-fold excess of oxygen is necessary for the production of the energy required for the biochemical processes that are unique to the brain, such as the synthesis (production) of neurotransmitters, their use and re-use. Each of these steps requires energy. An enormous amount of energy is also needed in the brain to operate the vast number of tiny 'pumps' that move key metal ions (particularly potassium and calcium) in and out of nerve cells – part of the so-called bioelectrical activity of the nervous system. Oxygen and all the basic materials for these biochemical and bioelectrical processes are transported and distributed in the brain by the cerebral blood flow (CBF).

A steady supply of energy is therefore critical for the brain to function properly. A deficient diet, a temporary lack of food (i.e. fewer carbo-hydrates to burn) or a lack of oxygen can all cause the brain to operate less efficiently. Under normal circumstances, there is a relatively large reserve of organic materials in the brain, but only a few minutes without oxygen can cause problems. Seven minutes of anoxia (absence of oxygen) can cause serious, often irreversible damage. And ten minutes or so without oxygen can be the cause of brain death, which is, in effect, the end of life.

The supply of oxygen to the brain tends to decrease with age. This may be caused by gradual blockage at key intersections in the blood supply system, owing to the accumulation of fatty deposits. This so-called sclerotic situation can eventually lead either to a massive stroke or to local mini-strokes in the brain capillaries – the multiple infarct dementia we referred to above, which is often confused with Alzheimer's. Fortunately, MID is relatively rare, affecting less than 0.6 per cent of the population aged over sixty-five. In addition, all muscles get weaker with age, and the heart, which is mostly muscle, becomes less efficient at pushing blood to the extremities (fingers and toes) and particularly to the brain. Incidentally, giraffes have a problem even in adulthood in maintaining an adequate blood supply to their brain, and seem to have evolved a special mechanism to ensure adequate cerebral blood flow. In humans, the local pulsations in the capillaries that distribute the blood throughout the brain also become less efficient with age as their walls lose flexibility.

Various attempts have been made to overcome the decrease of oxygen reaching the brain. An obvious method might be to breath oxygen from cylinders through an oxygen mask, but this does not appear to be either practical or effective in the long run. A more radical approach, tried some years ago in Boston, Massachusetts, was the use of hyperbaric oxygen. People suffering from memory loss were put inside a large, sealed vessel and subjected to a pressure of many atmospheres of oxygen. This was reported to have a small positive effect as measured by various tests, but the improvement was found to be minimal and transient. The loss of memory returned very soon after the patients resumed normal life outside the chamber, indicating that a more radical approach was needed. Obviously, the problem of a reduced oxygen supply to the brain cannot be cured by one or two hyperbaric treatments.

As might be expected, many pharmaceutical firms have spent a great deal of time and money in looking for effective, safe drugs for the treatment of memory loss, but with little success. For many years, one of the most effective medications for treating some forms of AAMI has been Hydergine, a complex molecule, synthesized and marketed by the Swiss firm Sandoz (now part of Artemis). As will be discussed in the next chapter, there was, for some time, a suggestion that this drug improved brain metabolism, i.e. increased its energy level, but there has never been a really satisfactory explanation for its action.

The simplest approach to increasing oxygen supply to the brain is, of course, exercise, in any form that will increase blood flow and not over-exert the heart. A great deal has been written on the effects of different types of exercise, from jogging and cycling to various forms of treadmill. For the elderly – that is, those over sixty – probably the best form of exercise is daily, rapid walking. However, although this may be a simple and effec-tive method, the problems of available time and boredom remain.

The second group of reasons for the loss of memory in adults can be considered to be the effects of medication, drugs or alcohol. Alcohol (known as ethanol or ethyl alcohol to chemists) has a curious role in brain function. It is, of course, an excellent fuel and can temporarily replace carbohydrates in the body for the production of energy, par-ticularly in the head. However, even in relatively modest doses, it tends to replace other forms of 'nutrition', reducing the appetite and thereby depleting the body of essential fats, vitamins (such as thiamine) and minerals. This can eventually lead to death – one of the classic, tragic outcomes of heavy drinking. The steady drinking of alcohol in large amounts has the well-known, immediate consequences of loss of con-centration, problems with balance and impaired sense of timing. Eventu-ally drinking alcohol starts to destroy the liver and parts of the brain. A serious and ultimately fatal brain disease, known as Korsakoff's syn-drome, is due to the erosion of parts of the brain in alcoholics.

On the more positive side, there is no doubt that a modest amount of alcohol improves mood, which, particularly in the elderly, helps over-come the lack of interest or motivation that is essential for a good working brain. In addition, small amounts of alcohol, imbibed daily, can have a beneficial, fluidizing effect on the membranes of brain cells, as will be discussed in Chapter 6. Much, however, seems to depend on the personality and the habits of those involved.

The effect of addictive drugs on the brain is complex and, on the whole, harmful. Some hallucinatory drugs, taken once or twice, may give the impression of improving 'awareness', sensitivity to input and perhaps even memory. There is, however, no evidence that any such drug actually does improve either learning or memory.

Other medications, either artificial or extracted from plants, of which there are many thousands, usually have little effect on the central nervous system unless they are specifically designed to do so. Most drugs are prevented from entering the brain by the blood–brain barrier (BBB), and are consequently safe to take at the prescribed dose. Some medications do, however, have the side-effects of reducing awareness or attention, and can cause sleepiness, which has obvious drawbacks in situations where maximal concentration is needed, such as studying or driving. Attention is usually drawn to this contra-indication on the packaging of certain medications.

The so-called CNS (central nervous system) drugs are designed specifically to enter the brain cells and deal with various types of disorder – epilepsy, schizophrenia, Parkinsonism, mania, clinical depression, etc. Taken at the recommended doses, they usually do not affect memory in any serious way. The one exception seems to be the 'minor tranquillizers' or diazepines, which have been shown to cause amnesia or forgetting when taken over long periods. This is particularly serious in the elderly, who often take tranquillizers to deal with anxiety. In addition, many such tranquillizers are commonly taken by people in certain stressful professions, who may not know of the proven effects on memory or alertness. Here, as in the case of most pharmaceutical drugs, every effective medication inevitably has its side-effects. It has been said that medication that has no side effects whatsoever, usually doesn't work. The rule of thumb is that the advantages must be weighed against the risk – an evaluation that can be done only by a physician or psychiatrist.

An important effect of normal ageing on memory is that affecting neural or brain chemistry, or more accurately, the biochemical processes occurring in the nerve cell network. Over time, inevitable changes take place both on the surface and inside neurons. It is remarkable that, on the whole, these changes do not become apparent for the first fifty years or so. However, during the second fifty years, they can and do become increasingly noticeable. There is an increasing awareness among neuro-scientists that some of these changes are not accidental, but are somehow planned or programmed in the DNA of nerve cells. There may, in fact, be a mechanism that shuts off the continuous replenishment of the contents of nerve cells – planned apoptosis, or cell death, which will cause a reduction of the efficiency of the brain over time.

The gradual running down of brain cell activity may occur inside the neurons, which although consisting largely of water, contain an enormous variety of proteins and other substances. Thousands of these proteins are enzymes, and related giant molecules, such as receptors and transporters, are continuously being resynthesized in order to promote and control nearly all the biochemical processes taking place in living things. However, in the course of time, the newly formed enzymes may undergo slight changes in shape, resulting in their becoming less effective. These changes are due to small mistakes in their structure as they are recycled, i.e. broken down by other enzymes, by various types of radiation, or by active chemical species, such as free radicals, and then rebuilt. These small mistakes in the structure of enzymes cause them to lose their potency.

Of the hundreds of proteins that have key roles in the brain, some have a direct effect on memory – the recording of information, its retention or retrieval. One effect is to reduce the speed with which enzyme-catalysed reactions take place even by a few per cent, which will slow down one of the critical chemical processes involved with memory. There is at present no simple way of reversing this trend and improving the performance of enzymes, particularly those inside the cells of the central nervous system, which is so carefully protected by nature from outside intervention.

The other changes with age are those connected to the outside of neurons, the membranes or 'envelopes' that surround all living cells, including those in the brain. Most cells, such as those of the liver, are fairly resistant to change. In the cardiovascular system there is a constant surveillance of blood cells, and the defective ones are either destroyed or removed from the blood stream. However, the brain is a sort of 'protected area', guarded by the blood–brain barrier. Only those materials needed for the proper functioning of the CNS can get into the neurons, such as water, oxygen, glucose, various amino acids and their derivatives. A very important group of materials that can also get into brain cells fairly easily are lipids – relatively inert fatty substances which, among other things, provide the bulk of the material for cell walls and the insulating cover of nerve fibres.

Nerve cell membranes, like all cell membranes, are found to consist of a mixture of two classes of lipids – phospholipids (lecithin is a well-known example) and cholesterol. Together they form a tight protective jacket around the contents of the cell. Into this oily envelope a whole array of proteins are embedded: many of these are enzymes, others are receptors (biological antennae), and some are channels or pores through which salts, such as those of potassium or calcium, enter and exit. In the brain, packed with millions of neurons, these membranes, which have the consistency of honey, provide an oily barrier or boundary between one cell and the next.

The overall complex chemical composition of each membrane is determined genetically, and it is constantly being renewed or repaired with very little variation. However, over the course of many years, it appears that the amount of cholesterol in brain cell membranes rises very gradually, since cholesterol from the blood can eventually find its way to brain cell membranes, stick there and modify them. Cholesterol is a material that makes membranes more rigid, whereas phospholipids make them looser or more fluid. Gradually and insidiously, these membranes become stiffer due to an accumulation of minute amounts of cholesterol, and the enzymes and other proteins embedded in them change shape or position and become slightly less efficient.

It is a fact that in most biological systems the efficiency of enzymes is at a maximum, having reached their best performance after millions of years of evolution, so that any change is usually for the worse. The changes in membrane-bound enzymes in the brains of older people, as well as in ageing rats, monkeys and other animals that have been investigated, apparently slow down many brain-related processes, such as speed of reaction, acuity of vision and hearing, and (what concerns us most) the search for and recall of information. Exactly which enzymes and receptors are affected and how they are changed with age is still being worked out.

As will be discussed in Chapter 6 methods are now being tried to reverse this process in the brains of animals by diet, using the fluidizing component of membranes – phospholipids – such as a special kind of lecithin. After a few days of such treatment, the memory of aged rats seems to improve when tested in a Morris water maze. A three-year-old rat considered to be equivalent to a seventy- or eighty-year-old person, and the time taken to reach sanctuary by swimming in a maze may not be the best test of human memory, but the treatment has potential and its effect on elderly people is currently being determined. Such clinical tests take a great deal of time, effort and money, however, and it may take some time before the results are known.

Finally, there is a miscellaneous group of adverse effects on memory that are mostly connected to damage to specific areas of the brain. These include the effects of wounds in people due to accidents or wars, and deliberate lesions made in the nervous systems or brains of various types of organism from sea slugs to monkeys. Another set of brain-damaging effects are caused by viruses, such as HIV, which can penetrate into the brain and cause dementia. Various environmental chemicals or toxins also have deleterious effects on brain function. They include many pesticides, metals such as cadmium (the problem of aluminium has already been discussed) and gases from industrial processes, as well as radiation from natural or artificial sources. A great deal of research, mainly by industrial and environmental psychologists, is ongoing in this area.

There is evidence to suggest that the personality of the Spanish painter Francisco de Goya changed dramatically in his forty-sixth year. In 1792 he became giddy, nauseous and partially deaf, and he eventually died of a massive stroke in 1828. His style of painting changed in those dramatic years from the conventional style of the nineteenth century, to the brooding, gloomy pictures of his later years. This was apparently due to severe mercury or lead poisoning caused by the way he mixed his pigments. This is a dramatic example of the effect of a toxin on the central nervous system.

On the other hand there are many creative people, including painters, who were active until a very old age. Titian was past eighty when he painted one of his best pictures, *The Battle of Lepanto*, and Picasso, as is well known, was particularly creative towards the end of his life. Frank Lloyd Wright, the famous architect designed one of his most innovative buildings, the Guggenheim Museum in New York at the age of eighty-eight. An excellent example, amongst composers, is Verdi, who at age eighty-one composed one of his best operas – *Falstaff*. These talented people may be unusual but they indicate that creativity, great skill, and many aspects of a good memory, are not confined to the 'middle years' as long as one remains healthy and active.

The effects of various diseases on memory has been studied. For instance, hypertension and the medications usually taken to correct high blood pressure do not seem to have any adverse effects. Neurological diseases such as epilepsy and multiple sclerosis do not affect memory specifically. Brain tumours do, of course, have a considerable negative effect, depending on their size and location. This is particularly serious when very small cancerous growths affect blood supply.

A major reason for the loss of memory with age is the fact that brain cells are constantly dying. The number that disappear each day – in the tens of thousands – seems horrendous, but it is almost negligible when compared to the billions of neurons in a normal, healthy, human brain. The loss of brain cells is a slow, insidious process, quite distinct from the rapid decline in Alzheimer patients. The loss of neurons is not uniform. Some areas, such as the prefrontal lobes (just behind the forehead and eyes), the visual and auditory cortices, and, of course, the hippocampus, are the most affected. The net result is that the brain shrinks by 10–20 per cent by the age of ninety, becomes lighter, and contains more cerebrospinal fluid.

Among the other causes, two psychological reasons for loss of memory must be mentioned: stress and depression. The loss of memory caused by stress is not fully understood, like the condition itself. Stress and its relationship to psychosomatic disorders – that is, the effects of psychological situations on essential biological processes in the body – are hard to study in humans due to the very large differences between one individual and another. Even animal models of stress are hard to compare or quantify. In any case, people under stress, for whatever reason (noise, weather, personal problems, etc.), seem to have difficulty in remembering even fairly simple things. Since stress is related to hormone levels, this seems to indicate that an imbalance in certain hormones, however slight, has a direct connection to memory. How and why this complicated situation occurs is still being sorted out.

Depression is also known to affect memory. Some forms of depression are, in fact, often confused with memory loss, since any lack of interest or attention can confound the results of tests. This problem is discussed in the next chapter in connection with memory-improving drugs. The use of anti-depressants can make matters more complicated. If such drugs are withheld even for a relatively short time, the ability to concentrate, to remember, or even to learn new things returns.

Another major reason for memory loss in ordinary people is disuse, perhaps as a result of retirement, boredom or too much reliance on alternative methods of recording information, from notebooks to computers. Plato is supposed to have said that writing is deleterious to the mind. In contrast, practising to remember things is perhaps one way of keeping the brain active. We will discuss some of the techniques devised to improve memory in the next chapter.

CHAPTER SIX

Regaining one's memory

'If any one faculty of our nature may be called more wonderful than the rest, I do think it is memory ... [which] is sometimes so retentive and so reliable, so obedient – and at others so bewildered and so weak.'
Fanny Price in *Mansfield Park* (Jane Austen, 1775–1817)

Regaining or improving one's memory implies that things can get better than they are now. This can mean objective improvement, as determined by carefully conducted tests of the ability to recall names, recognize faces or repeat numbers; alternatively, there is a subjective feeling that one's memory is somehow better than it was – a sense of well-being, part of the 'feel-good factor'. The problem of standard memory tests in people is that of comparison. Is a person's memory 'better' than it was at some previous moment in time – a day, a week, a year or a decade ago? Alternatively, is it better or worse as compared to that of other people of the same sex, age and background? When testing groups of people, ideally one should compare 'controls', who have the same age and education, eat the same food, sleep the same amount of time, etc., with 'experimentals'. In the extreme, one should, in fact, compare identical twins brought up together all their lives, as had been done in some genetic studies on mental disorders such as schizophrenia. One can do this with inbred rats, but it is very difficult to extend it to people.

Neither approach to studying the improvement of memory is ideal, since so many other factors may be involved. Some of the variables can be controlled, such as the depth and length of sleep before the tests of memory, the effect of meals, the time of day, and the conditions of the test itself: the size of the room and even the personality of the tester or investigator. Others are more difficult to control, such as personal problems of worry or stress. There is also the confusion as to which of the many types of memory system is being tested. As discussed in Chapter 4 there is memory for faces, for music, for words or for places – and the improvement can occur to a different extent in each case.

The remarkable memory of most professional musicians for whole operas, symphonies and concertos has already been discussed. However, the memory for faces and names seems to be highly developed among other specific groups of people, such as diplomats and doormen. This is probably because their future employment prospects are often dependent on their ability to remember faces and names. Diplomats and doormen apparently make an extra effort to pay attention, to note small differences in features that make a face more easily recalled, and perhaps almost instinctively use mnemonics (memory-improving techniques) for associating a face and perhaps other physical features – such as height, bulk, style of dress or the amount of hair on the face – with the name. There is no doubt that, apart from the importance of relating names to faces, the ability to do so rapidly, even after a very long time, has a gratifying effect on the person being recognized. It could be that people with a good memory for faces are attracted to these occupations.

A good memory for words is characteristic of actors who can remember whole scripts of plays. Learning texts by heart is an essential skill in the performing arts, particularly in the theatre. Many actors claim that their phenomenal memory is 'state related' – they rely on cues from other actors, both in words and in their position on the stage, and often do not remember their lines if something is changed. In order to learn new scripts, many actors claim that they deliberately convert a string of words into imaginary positions along a well-known route. Subsequent recall is then made easier by just following that imaginary route and picking up the words or phrases in their correct sequence. Converting memory for words into memory for well-known places has been a popular technique from the time of the Greek orator Simonides to the present day.

It has often been said that the key to a good memory is paying attention. This selective form of arousal has been studied extensively in animals, usually laboratory rats, as well as in people. The debate about how the process of paying attention occurs has long occupied the minds of psychologists, who first realized that it concerns the selection of a certain train of thought from a large number of alternatives. Concentration, or focusing, is a key factor here, implying withdrawal of thought or consciousness from a range of other possibilities in order to deal effectively with one of them.

The opposite is known as being confused, dazed or scatterbrained. The cause of one's divided attention can be external stimuli, such as music or loud noises or internal events, such as random trains of thought, or even anxiety caused by unsuccessful attempts to retrieve information – the 'tip of the tongue' phenomenon. This problem is best overcome by relaxation – by trying to think of something else. Worrying about an elusive name, word or tune only makes it more difficult to remember.

The ability to pay attention varies between individuals and is based on experience, or on developing a strategy. In order to pay attention, one first has to perceive and identify the item, distinguish it from others, and concentrate on it. It is then easier to remember by means of association with other items – an important feature of the memory system. An interesting illustration is the 'cocktail party' phenomenon where, in a crowded, noisy gathering, a person in one corner of the room can often notice or even listen to a conversation of particular interest taking place in another remote corner. Here, attention has usually been reinforced or strengthened by overhearing a key word, such as one's own name. This trigger causes attention to be focused and overrides the much louder discussion taking place all around.

This link between attention and consciousness has been the subject of many recent books. It appears that the human brain is limited at any one moment by the number of stimuli (or items) that can be attended to or processed (see 'chunking' in Chapter 4). Psychologists have addressed many questions. How does selective attention operate? What portion of the incoming information can be attended to? Is the control of attention voluntary? The latter is a problem encountered by many teachers and lecturers facing a large class. What happens to unattended irrelevant information? Can a person attend to two things at once? How long can attention be maintained? This is one of the considerations of advertisers on radio and television, who are concerned with attention spans to make their pitch. And finally, are there different types of attention, as there are of sensory memory?

A great many very ingenious laboratory experiments have been devised for the study of attention and particularly selective attention – such as whether the colour of an object is perceived or remembered when the subjects are required only to identify its shape. Conflicting or irrelevant information in the form of words or sounds can be produced through loudspeakers or earphones to test whether a 'filtering process' exists in which attention can be paid to one form of information against a background of irrelevant 'noise'.

The length of time for which attention can be maintained is known sometimes as vigilance, and is important in the study of the working hours and schedules of air-traffic controllers and radar operators. There are obviously considerable individual differences, but it has been found that attention in complex situations is a skill that can be taught by training and improved by experience. Air-traffic controllers, for instance, can be taught to develop better ways of allocating their attention, and to use strategies for coping with an overload of information. This is the basis of the many books designed to improve memory through the development of attention skills. An example of these skills is the classic parlour game Pelmanism, in which a pack of playing cards is spread face downwards on a table. Each player turns over a card and, if he can remember and find a similar card, removes the pair. If the two cards turned over are not the same, they are turned face down again. The winner is the player who has the most pairs of cards at the end of the game, and usually the one who can concentrate best. Variations of Pelmanism are the basis of many commercial, memory-improving techniques.

An unusual method of memory enhancement is the use of hypnosis, which is the induction of a state of relaxation caused by suggestion, monotonous music or the motion of pendulums. It differs from sleep in that the subject remains capable of responding to instructions and questions. It has been used in the past by some psychoanalysists and more recently, under certain circumstances, by forensic or police investigators. There are various explanations for the ability of some people, but not all, to remember under hypnosis details of things that happened days or even years earlier, which they appear to have forgotten. The details and clarity of the memories vary considerably from person to person. It has been suggested that hypnosis merely relaxes the subject or perhaps helps in the association of details of the incident, particularly if it was an unpleasant or very dramatic one. Whatever the explanation, it seems that remembering under hypnosis can and does occur. However, the process of hypnosis itself is not entirely understood, and the experiments conducted to understand its effect on memory (or rather the retrieval of information) are not conclusive. There is also some controversy about the use of such techniques by police investigators for solving crimes or extracting information from those in custody. Hypnosis and sleep are somehow related and 'sleep learning' enjoyed a brief fashion in the 1960s. Devices were sold that were reported to teach a foreign language, key facts in chemistry or important dates in history using a specially recorded tape attached to an earphone placed under or in a pillow. Various methods were used to ensure that the machine was only switched on, automatically, during specific types of sleep. However, no learning could be detected after many years of trials, so sleep learning machines have virtually disappeared. As with memory drugs, it was reported at the time that the more a machine cost, the more effective it was said to be. In fact, it appears that it is not possible to learn anything by simple auditory methods during sleep.

Physiological methods of improving memory, such as the use of hyperbaric oxygen chambers, were discussed in Chapter 5. Most of these methods are concerned with increasing cerebral blood flow or raising heart rate through walking and exercise. But owing to the great interest in memory, particularly loss of memory, it is not surprising that a great deal of attention has been given to alternative, pharmacological methods, where certain key important chemicals in the brain are manipulated by medication.

The list of chemicals suggested for improving memory – both natural products and artificially designed molecules – runs into many hundreds, but there is very little solid evidence for the efficacy of most of them. Many of these drugs or treatments have not been tested under rigorous conditions, either on experimental animals (rats or monkeys), or on people. An important factor that was ignored in early studies on memory-enhancing medication in humans were the psychological effects. For whatever reason, people involved in experiments on memory feel an excitement and tension in being 'memory improvement' pioneers. This can negate the disinterest and apathy that envelops the lives of elderly people, who are the natural candidates for such experiments. Nowadays, as a result of 'Helsinki' laws, all subjects for experiments or tests for new medication – in the western world, at least – must give their 'informed consent'. This means agreeing to participate after being told all the details and problems involved, which may cause a psychologically based improvement.

There were reports in the 1950s and 1960s that scientists in Canada and elsewhere had succeeded in improving the memory of the inhabitants of old people's homes by giving them yeast RNA tablets. The investigators seem to have ignored the fact that any strands of RNA molecules contained in such tablets would rapidly be destroyed by the acids and enzymes in the body, particularly in the stomach. In any case, large molecules such as RNA would have had great difficulty in penetrating the blood–brain barrier, in entering brain cells or in influencing behaviour. There was no simple explanation why ingested RNA, extracted from yeast, should help memory in humans, and the whole idea has since been dropped. For some time there was a lingering suggestion that some of the components of RNA may be able to improve memory by supplying essential nutrients, such as phosphate. But even this idea has now disappeared.

Another interesting aspect of memory drugs is the fact that the cost of such tablets is not trivial. There are many anecdotal reports of successful memory improvement made by people who obtained various tablets and tried them. However, it turns out very frequently that the more expensive a treatment is, the more effective people believe it to be. Obviously, so the thinking goes, something that is expensive (or unpleasant) must be effective. This is the reason, I believe, why such optimistic reports were made some years ago in Germany and Switzerland on the rejuvenating effects of extremely expensive treatments involving extracts from foetal animal glands. This problem has dogged much of the reporting on the effectiveness of memory-improving drugs.

In the past two decades, memory drugs have been tested using the 'double-blind' procedure in order to eliminate any subjective distortion of the results. In other words, experimental and control groups of subjects are matched in number, gender, age, mental condition and even diet, and are tested for memory using one of a number of standard questionnaires. The controls receive a 'placebo', i.e. a harmless, tasteless, ineffective substitute such as chalk, which looks exactly like the actual medication given to the experimental group. Before the test, all participants are given a code number, and all those involved in the test use these code numbers throughout, so that they do not known which participants were given the 'real thing' and which a placebo. Only after the tests of memory are finally completed are the results for the experimentals and the controls compared. A statistical analysis is usually required to get final results, particularly if the number of patients or the difference between experimentals and controls is small.

A serious problem in the evaluation of many memory drugs is that the elderly people used in the tests often subsist on a poor diet, so that any form of food additive can appear to improve their memory simply by increasing alertness; they are also likely to improve because some concern is being given to their welfare (as happened with the RNA tablets). This may be the reason why the original reports of the effects of amino acids (such as glutamic acid, glycine and serine) and of various sugars on memory in both rats and people appeared at the time to be positive. These substances probably contributed to general metabolism and protein synthesis, but do not, when carefully tested in rats or humans, have any specific effects on the nervous system or memory. An exception may be the derivative of one amino acid, serine, known as phosphatidylserine or PS, that is reported to have some effect in improving memory, and is available in health food stores as a food additive. It probably works by altering nerve cell membranes. Glucose, at certain doses, is also said to improve learning in rats, although this may be caused by a general improvement in nutrition or activity. Peptides, a generic term for relatively short strings of amino acids, have the advantage that they can often penetrate the blood–brain barrier and enter nerve cells. Many of these substances are also hormones, heart stimulants or involved in stress or fear. Although there have been ups and downs in the use of peptides for memory enhancement, there does not seem to be much enthusiasm for using them at present.

An interesting example of a memory-improving drug is a substance called 'pemoline', which was briefly in fashion some years ago. It was eventually found that the magnesium used to make up the tablet has a small positive effect on the well-being of both humans and rats. Magnesium is required for many enzymes, but when pemoline is used by itself, it is apparently ineffective. Among the more dramatic possibilities for memory improvement is strychnine, a classic poison used since Roman times, and a component of some medicines or 'tonics' used in the nineteenth century. It is now known that in very small doses, strychnine has a stimulating effect on some components of the nervous system. This effect is very small and transient, however, and the dangers of using such a poisonous substance for memory improvement far outweigh any value it may have.

Nicotine and other alkaloids, with less lethal effects, might one day turn out to be very effective. It has been reported that in small doses (a single cigarette), nicotine does sometimes improve memory as measured by various tests. This is a complex problem connected to the ability of nicotine to interfere with the acetylcholine system, triggering off a cascade of biochemical processes that may temporarily strengthen the link between neurons. The relaxation or feeling of well-being obtained by some people from smoking even one cigarette may also have an effect. In contrast, there is no doubt that 'hard' drugs (morphine, LSD, cocaine, etc.), apart from threatening addiction, gradually cause irreversible changes in the brain that inevitably have a negative effect on memory. Damage to intercellular communication between nerve cells is not easily repaired, even after fairly long periods of abstinence or 'drying out'.

Alcohol, often compared to the other mind-altering drugs, is equally devastating in its long-term effects (see Chapter 5). However, there is evidence that when alcohol is taken in small amounts, immediately after learning some verbal or visual material, memory is actually improved. There are various possible explanations for this observation. The simplest one is that the alcohol provides extra 'fuel' for some of the biochemical processes involved in either learning or memory. This does not seem likely because the amount of alcohol is so small. Alternatively, it has been suggested that alcohol might stimulate consolidation of the memory-trace by raising blood-glucose levels. Another suggestion is that alcohol is a cell-membrane fluidizer (see later). It has the advantage of being able to penetrate the blood–brain barrier, and could therefore improve one of the stages of learning or memory by increasing communication between neurons. Finally, there is the well-known effect of alcohol on improving mood, which is certainly involved in the process of learning. The difficulties of designing conclusive experiments on the effects of small amounts of alcohol are considerable, so this topic remains an interesting though inconclusive subject for research.

An intriguing family of drugs that were popular in the 1970s were named 'no-otropics' by their proponents. The name was based on the Greek for 'knowledge improving'. They were all related to an odd-shaped small molecule, given the trade name Piracetam by a Belgian pharmaceutical company. Piracetam, taken as a pill, appears to penetrate the brain easily, but although various explanations for its action have been given, they have generally been unconvincing. A number of large pharmaceutical companies have prepared very similar compounds, slight variations of the original Piracetam structure. But it appears that the results were not sufficiently successful or consistent to warrant their large-scale production or sale. Although no-otropics are non-toxic at the recommended doses, the fact that no mechanism for their action has yet been found is probably one of the reasons why they are not more popular. However, Piracetam is still marketed, and a research group in Germany has very recently shown that it may act by changing the flexibility or fluidity of nerve-cell membranes, again improving communication in the neural network.

A very popular medication that is claimed to alleviate recent memory impairment is Hydergine, which is also reputed to deal with fatigue, anxiety, depression, confusion, dizziness, lack of self-care and unsociability. Hydergine is a complicated molecule of the alkaloid family, but its mode of action is not clear. So far it has not been approved specifically for memory improvement, although there is some evidence that it may improve brain metabolism. This emphasizes the importance of a good supply of oxygen to the brain (see Chapter 5). Hydergine has been a great success commercially and apparently has almost no side effects.

Another approach to memory improvement has been an attempt to bolster the neurotransmitter system or systems related to memory.

Acetylcholine has long been a favourite transmitter for those dealing with the chemistry of the brain and particularly memory. Many attempts have been made to increase the amount of this transmitter in the brain. Acetylcholine itself is expensive, very unstable and rapidly destroyed by enzymes in the stomach and bloodstream, and it would have great difficulty in penetrating the blood–brain barrier. One approach is to supply the body by mouth, in the form of pills or liquid concoctions, with a precursor, one of the substances from which it is made in living systems. It has been assumed that this material would be carried by the bloodstream to reach the brain and the hippocampus, the relay station of memory formation. When using animals, usually rats, it is more convenient and generally more effective to deliver medication inter-peritoneally (ip), the technical term for injection into the stomach cavity. In both animals and people, acetylcholine is made in nerve cells from acetic acid (acetate), a very common material in the body, and choline, a substance almost specific to the brain. In tests, many animals and some humans were injected or fed choline, but this treatment did not appear to improve the memory of rats, normal people or those with age-associated memory impairment (AAMI). Choline also has the disadvantage of imparting a distinctly fishy smell to the subjects taking it, which has not encouraged its use by people. Related compounds with slight variations in their chemical structure have also been tried, but without success. One of these is Deanol (diethanolamine), which resembles part of the choline molecule, but does not seem to show any positive effects.

The precursors of a number of other neurotransmitters have also been tried, in the hope that they would enter the brain, improve neuro-transmission and enhance memory. The list includes phenylalanine and tyrosine, which are sold in health food stores and pharmacies. Both are amino acids and precursors of dopamine, which is an important neurotransmitter essential to proper brain function, particularly atten-tion, motion and mood. However, in properly conducted tests, no specific effect on memory has ever been demonstrated. Various vitamins and some anti-oxidants – substances that prevent damage to cell com-ponents – have also been tried, so far with no significant effects on memory, although this approach does have potential.

It would be pointless to list individually all the compounds tried both in academia and by pharmacological companies which have not been effective in improving memory. If any of them had improved memory, they would have been much more widely advertised and used. In fact, it has been said, rather cynically, that any memory-enhancing drug that has been discussed at a conference dealing with brain pharmacology either is toxic or doesn't work.

Until recently, there has been a frustrating silence in brain research circles on the whole subject of the improvement of memory. This is due partly to the difficulties in testing drugs for their specific effects, and partly to the fact that the authorities that license or approve the use of medications (such as the Food and Drug Administration, or FDA, in the United States) have not, until very recently, accepted ageing as a disease. They have made the point that, unlike cancer, measles or malaria it is very hard to prove, unequivocally, that the loss of memory has been 'cured'. The change in attitude has arisen from public pressure and the increasing concern with Alzheimer's disease. As discussed in Chapter 5, there has been a considerable improvement in identifying 'early' Alzheimer's disease patients using non-invasive techniques such as PET and fMRI.

The difficulty of distinguishing between benign (age-related) memory loss and early Alzheimer's is slowly being overcome. One of the first drugs to be taken seriously for the treatment of AD was Tacrine and related compounds. It was finally approved by the FDA and shown to be able to increase the concentration of acetylcholine in the brain by blocking the enzyme that destroys it. This provides a possible mechanism of action, which is essential for the approval of any new medication. Tacrine has been found to increase the acetylcholine in the brain in a fairly non-specific way, but as AD progresses and more cholinergic (i.e. acetylcholine-containing) cells die, the efficacy of this medication falls off. Tacrine has fairly serious side-effects, causing liver and other forms of damage, which limits its use for an extended period.

Many new drugs for treating AD are now in the process of being tested, at least on animals, and may soon be available for the treatment of people. One is based on the use of compounds from the ampakine family, which can increase the flow of calcium into brain cells. Calcium is known to trigger many biochemical reactions, such as the release of the amino acid, glutamic acid. Although glutamic acid has no effect when taken as a pill, there are some suggestions that ampakines might improve the health and survival of nerve cells. It is hoped that the intense search for a cure for AD will soon produce a viable treatment for the improvement of memory in the public at large. Many of these drugs are closely guarded secrets in pharmaceutical labs, which makes it very difficult to get any hard information at present.

An entirely different but, I believe, promising approach is to tackle the structure of neurons themselves. Nerve cells are surrounded by membranes that change very slowly with age. As discussed in Chapter 5, over time the membranes of many cells in both rats and people become more rigid. This may be caused by changes in chemical composition or attack by free radicals, the very reactive parts of molecules that attack many biological materials. Although the changes in nerve cell membranes may be very small, they can cause profound alterations in transmitter release and other key chemical processes. It has been shown that the membranes of almost all cells consist of a neatly organized mixture of cholesterol and a number of 'fluidizing' phospholipids. The most common phospholipid is lecithin (PC), about which much has been written in recent years. In all cells, particularly neurons, the cholesterol is the cause of stiffness in the membrane, whereas the greater the proportion of phospholipids, the more fluid is the membrane.

Measurements of the brains of old experimental animals (two- and three-year-old rats or mice), as well as the brains of people post-mortem, show that over time and for unknown reasons, the relative amount of cholesterol increases, causing cell membranes to become stiffer – the consistency of treacle or molasses. However, when old animals are injected or fed with lecithin, their nerve cell membranes are partially restored to their original 'youthful' state. One of the complications in this area of research has been that lecithin is a collective term for a whole family of very similar materials. The relatively cheap soy lecithin, which is extracted from soya beans, has been readily available for some time in health food stores, but does not, so far, seem to be effective. Another, more specialized member of this family, egg lecithin, extracted from egg yolks by a simple industrial process, shows great promise. When egg lecithin is taken as a pill, it is exposed to enzymes and acids in the digestive tract and bloodstream, and largely destroyed *en route* to the brain. However, if egg lecithin is contained in a suspension of small droplets of a mixture of lipids, it seems to survive better and eventually reaches the brain. This (patented) mixture is non-toxic and is shortly to be tested on elderly people suffering from memory loss. Preliminary experiments have shown that when three-year-old rats, who have lost their ability to learn how to negotiate and remember a simple maze, are treated with egg lecithin for some weeks, they learn and remember how to cope almost as well as young (nine-month-old) animals. However, the way in which egg lecithin works is still not entirely clear.

The maze referred to here is not one of those complicated wooden mazes or mechanical learning devices, such as the Skinner box, that used to be all the rage in departments of psychology and pharmacology specializing in rat behaviour. Nowadays life has become much easier for the experimenters, who can test rats for learning and memory in a 'Morris water maze'. This is a large round, shallow pool or tank of water, to which a milky substance is added to make it opaque. Somewhere in this pool, below the surface, a platform or brick is placed which cannot be seen by a swimming rat. When the rat is placed in the water, it must swim around until it finds this 'sanctuary' by trial and error. In the course of repeated trials, a rat's performance improves as it gradually learns the fastest way to reach the platform and, importantly, to stay there. Young rats can learn to negotiate a Morris water maze easily and remember it from one day to the next using visual clues from the surroundings – the shape of the room, the position of the lights in the ceiling, etc. Old rats, or those with brain damage, have great difficulties. They often go on swimming round and round aimlessly, almost to exhaustion, and have to be rescued. In nearly all current work in rats on learning and memory, Morris water mazes are used. Perhaps this technique could be used to test a new memory drug on elderly people, by measuring the time it takes them to find a hidden platform in a swimming pool full of milk.

We have so far discussed memory enhancement, or improvement of the memory, in the elderly. One day these methods and medications might be used by university students and even school children for helping them remember their homework. So far, whenever such drugs have been tested on young people (or even young animals), very little improvement in memory or learning has been observed. This probably indicates that the normal brain has evolved to function at its optimum and cannot easily be improved. However, the possibility now exists of improving brain performance as well as memory by genetic engineering. This raises serious moral and ethical problems, which will be discussed in Chapter 7.

It is also possible to deliberately reduce certain specific aspects of memory by medication. I have mentioned the disruptive effects of alcohol and drug addiction, but there are more subtle distractions such as mood, noise and pain. The use of memory blockers has recently been suggested for the treatment of traumas caused by sexual assault, particularly in children, or by terrorist bombings, car accidents or even ethnic cleansing. Whether this is a good thing or not, and when, where and how such treatment should be used to bolster psychotherapy and counselling, is debatable. Memory-suppressing drugs are popularly known as 'bleach'. This name is based on a science fiction screenplay written by a student in New York, which deals with manipulating memory. One can envision the bleach approach being used for more sinister purposes, such as self-treatment by potential rapists and mur-derers in order to reduce their inhibitions and blank out the memories of their crimes.The question will then arise as to whether such criminals are accountable. These and other troubling scenarios arising from the manipulation of memory are no longer so far-fetched.

Finally, there are behavioural or psychological approaches to improv-ing memory. Many hundreds of books deal with techniques for memory improvement in people. The use of various mnemonic tricks started with Simonides (see Chapter 4) and continued through classical and medieval times, as described in Frances Yates' wonderful book, *The Art of Memory*. In the present day, such methods include the sing-song repetition and body swaying used by rabbinical teachers, and the intense concentration demanded by Indian gurus.

As we saw in Chapter 4, the first serious experiments in this field were made by Hermann Ebbinghaus a hundred years ago. By testing his own recall of nonsense syllables, he showed that 'cramming' does not help one's memory, but more often causes confusion. He also demonstrated the benefits of 'sleeping on it', which means that a good night's sleep helps consolidate information stored in short-term or working memory. His followers, mainly educational psychologists, showed that pausing now and then during learning to give time for 'consolidation' is another way to remember. There has been a great deal of activity in this area in the past forty years, concerned with improving the performance of pupils in school and the examination results of students in higher education.

Many books have been published in recent years on 'how to improve your memory'. All of them start with reassuring lists of simple symptoms: 'Do you misplace keys or glasses? Do you have difficulty in finding your car in a car park? Can you remember shopping lists or recognize a friend in an unfamiliar setting?' They then move on to what is called 'serious memory loss', which includes forgetting appointments, telling the same stories to the same people, being unable to manage one's financial accounts, failing to recognize one's close relatives, being confused about the time of day, and sudden changes in personality. The best advice for dealing with these latter problems is to see a doctor – a geriatric specialist, a neurologist or a psychiatrist. The minor memory lapses can often be overcome by reducing stress or worry (which may not be easy), by establishing a daily routine, enriching one's social life, having a pet, eating properly and regularly, and taking some exercise.

As we saw in Chapter 5, loss of memory can be caused by head injuries, strokes and various neurological diseases such as Alzheimer's. In fact, about half of those suffering from very serious loss of memory actually have AD, about 20 per cent have multiple minor cerebral strokes, another 20 per cent have insufficient nutrition or an excessive intake of alcohol, and the final 10 per cent of people with memory loss are depressed, a situation that can be treated by psychotherapy and/or anti-depressants. An often overlooked cause of the loss of memory is the effect of medication taken for other reasons, such as problems with the heart, digestion, sleep or pain. The adverse effects on memory of diazepine tranquillizers has already been mentioned, but other drugs can also affect memory when the dose is too large or there is some interaction between two or more drugs.

But if nothing else is seriously wrong, what can one do about forgetfulness? All the available books, courses and systems recommend techniques based on memorizing lists, solving pencil and paper puzzles, answering questionnaires and even talking to oneself. A major problem is how to maintain one's attention and concentration, but there have been very few new ideas in this area for some time. An interesting approach is a system called 'memerobics', a mental analogy of aerobics, in which the learning stage is based on remembering details of a popular film series and reinforcement by testing, using amusing and creative questionnaires. The main advantage of linking the memory course to popular entertainment is that it introduces an element of fun and eliminates the boredom of standard mnemonic techniques.

As in many other situations, a combination of approaches probably works best – mild medication, proper diet, simple exercise and psychological effort. Together with general mental and social activity, this will probably help to improve the minds of those whose memory is not what it used to be. However, in the final analysis, it does not hurt to write things down or to ask, 'What did you say your name was?'

CHAPTER SEVEN

The future of memory research: problems and possibilities

'Today is more interesting than yesterday and tomorrow, more than today.'
(Herbert Louis Samuel, 1st Viscount Samuel, 1870–1963)

Research on the brain and on memory is expanding at a very rapid rate, and in the past fifty years the number of neuroscientists has increased from hundreds to tens of thousands. The pressure to produce original ideas and approaches to understanding memory are increasing all the time, partly through a genuine spirit of inquiry, but also perhaps encouraged by the possibility of fame and financial reward.

The lure of fame and fortune has very often ignored any consideration of ethics. For example, in recent years a drastic approach to memory loss in general, and to Alzheimer's disease in particular, has been the suggestion of transplanting cerebral tissue, i.e. implanting nerve cells into defective areas of the brain. This idea is based on the attempts to deal with another neurological problem, Parkinson's disease (PD), by transplantation. Although the basic causes of Parkinsonism are as yet unclear, it is a fact that the neurotransmitter dopamine is no longer produced in sufficient quantities in a specific area of the brain, the substantia nigra.

In the 1980s a limited number of PD patients, mainly in Sweden, Mexico and the USA, underwent fairly drastic operations in which dopaminergic (i.e. dopamine-producing) cells were implanted in or near their substantia nigra. The surgery consisted of boring a small hole in the skull of anaesthetized PD patients and injecting cells taken from the patients' own adrenal glands through a long needle. However, it turns out that the transplantation of nerve cells in humans is not at all simple, and that the number and source of the dopaminergic cells, as well as the exact site where they are deposited in the recipient brain, is very important. Apparently, nerve growth-promoting peptides and perhaps other factors are also needed.

The sources of neural cells for this procedure have been discussed extensively in scientific journals and conferences. Preliminary experiments on neural transplantation were first done on rats, although the animal model of Parkinsonism leaves much to be desired. In humans, the few operations done have not been encouraging. Cells from the patients' own adrenal glands were used in the human operations in order to simplify the problem of possible immunological rejection. It was later suggested that embryonic cells might be more effective, as had been found to be the case in rats. However, in most countries there is at present a ban on the use of tissue from aborted human foetuses. The third possible source of dopaminergic cells might have been cadavers (as has been done in the transplantation of corneas, kidneys and hearts), but this has not generated much enthusiasm since brain cells are particularly sensitive to the supply of oxygen and those from a recently deceased person would be most vulnerable. Finally, there has been a suggestion of growing the appropriate brain cells or tissue *in vitro*, i.e. in a glass or plastic dish with an adequate supply of nutrients and oxygen. However, the excitement over neural cell or tissue transplants in humans has been dampened by arguments about the ethical use of human embryonic tissue and the cost and practicality of the operations. This subject is currently fairly dormant, although the results of the operations done in the 1980s ranged from partial recovery to what was reported as 'a reduced requirement for medication'. The effects of these 'transplantations' were, however reported to wear off with time.

The idea of transplanting brain cells or even parts of brain in cases of PD led to an interest in using the technique for other neurological diseases, the foremost being Alzheimer's. There is at present no successful treatment for AD, and the pressure from sufferers, their families and the public in general to 'do something' has led to a re-examination of the possibility of transplants. Here, however, there is an additional serious problem: no specific area or structure in the brain is affected in AD. The characteristic plaques and tangles, typical of cell death or malfunction, are distributed fairly widely and are almost impossible to identify or locate in living brain tissue. There is also no really convincing animal model for AD. Some work has been done on aged rats (between two and three years old), which have difficulty in learning or remembering a water maze – a model for benign loss of memory, or AAMI. In some experiments, cholinergic (acetylcholine-containing) cells have been replaced or augmented in the hippocampus by cells taken from embryonic brain tissue or from very young rats, but the results have been inconclusive. At present there does not seem to be much future to this approach.

In all the discussions on the possibility of cerebral cell transplantation in people, it has been assumed that changes in the personality or character of the recipient are very unlikely – beyond, that is, the changes that sometimes occur as a result of serious brain surgery. However, if one day, not only isolated cells, but larger pieces of brain are successfully transplanted to repair damage caused by accidents, brain tumours or strokes, problems of personal identity could occur. This is still a theoretical question, since no one yet knows how many cells or how large a piece of brain is needed to cause a change in the character or characteristics of the recipient. In other words, will parts of 'my' brain inside 'your' head make you similar to me, or different from what you used to be?

No such experiments have yet been contemplated in humans, although some years ago it was reported that parts of the brain were transplanted successfully in dogs and monkeys. However, these results have been disputed and never repeated in any other laboratory. It seems very unlikely that such transplants will be possible because of practical problems, such as ensuring an adequate supply of oxygen to the transplanted tissue and surrounding area not only during the operation but also during recovery, i.e. until the transplant has been successfully integrated into the recipient brain. An equally difficult problem is how the myriad of blood capillaries and nerve processes connect up to ensure a viable and working brain. During foetal or early development, the brain is connected up in the correct pattern, so it has been suggested that this might be the case following transplantation. However, this is by no means certain. There is the further problem of immunological rejection – that tissue from an outside source might be incompatible with existing tissue. All these practical difficulties do not at present seem capable of resolution, so little attention has been paid to the ethical dilemmas involved.

Despite the practical difficulties of transplanting brain tissue, the idea is not entirely in the realm of science fiction, as has been shown by experiments on lower vertebrates, such as amphibians, which have a number of unique characteristics. Apart from metamorphosis (transition from tadpole to adult), amphibians are unique in that the supply of oxygen to the brain in adults occurs not only through the lungs and circulation, but also by direct diffusion through the skin. More importantly, the nerves of amphibians, unlike those of mammals, have an ability to grow and regenerate, although how this is done is still a matter of debate. Tailed newts and salamanders are particularly good candidates for transplantation experiments, since their metabolism is slow, their brain anatomy is well studied, they can be taught visual discrimination and suitable anaesthetics for surgery are available.

The amphibian brain consists of two large, almond-shaped lobes, the forebrain, which controls complex behaviour such as vision and taste, behind which are smaller mid- and hind-brains, firmly attached to the spinal cord. In an anaesthetized amphibian, the forebrain can be separated from the mid-brain and excised. When the forebrains of two newts are exchanged, after two or three weeks of recuperation, most animals begin to move, swim and eat, and appear no different from unoperated animals. Newts can be taught to distinguish between shapes (say, a black circle or triangle) marking alternate arms of a simple automated maze, by being rewarded with a morsel of food when they make the correct choice. After a few days, adult newts can make the correct choice about 80 per cent of the time, well above chance, and remember this for quite some time. The frontal lobes from the brains of adult newts that have been taught to distinguish circles from triangles can then be exchanged with those from untrained animals. Following two weeks or so of recovery, the 'trained' animals with lobes from an untrained animal seem to 'forget' how to distinguish shapes. On the other hand, when frontal lobes from trained animals are transplanted into untrained newts, the latter appear to be able to distinguish between circles and triangles without having to be trained. The simplest explanation for this is that some information – recognizing shapes and associating them with food – has been transferred. Alternatively, some hormone that increases attention or arousal may be involved.

There is still some argument whether these experiments show that specific changes in behaviour or knowledge can indeed be transplanted, even in amphibians. On the other hand, genetic engineering has become an established fact through the development of DNA splicing. This raises a whole series of ethical questions that are still being debated. During the course of millions of years, 'life' on planet Earth has evolved from self-replicating aggregates of large molecules in the primordial oceans, through tiny organisms with simple nerve nets, to invertebrates with ganglia and the many species of vertebrates with which we are familiar. Many of these have been used as models for various behavioural and cognitive functions in humans. There is, of course, no reason to believe that evolution by natural selection has ended, but we now have the possibility of diverting it, controlling it or speeding it up. This possibility is what is so worrying.

Some thirty years ago, Paul Maclean, in the USA, suggested that, in evolving to its present size and complexity, the human brain has retained the distinctive features and chemistry of various 'ancestors'. He argued that the structure of the adult human brain reflects our ancestral relationship to reptiles, to early mammals, and finally to late mammals, resulting in what he called the 'triune brain'. Maclean suggested that the central core, the so-called limbic system of the human brain, is reptilian, devoted entirely to self-preservation. Later, with the transition to warm blood, early mammals possessed emotions and cared for their offspring, and perhaps for one another. In higher mammals, this emotional brain was then covered by the outer layer of an 'executive' brain. The triune brain then evolved through time from those of rat-like animals with a smooth cortex to the intricate convolutions of humans with a full range of cognitive functions and abilities. The abilities that characterize humans required the development of new brain areas to enable abstract thinking, problem solving, the use of language, tool making, planning for the future, and the consciousness of self.

We now have the ability to alter the course of evolution. Examples of this ability, relevant to the theme of this book are the production of behavioural mutants, first in Drosophila (fruit flies), using radiation or chemicals, and now in mice. The DNA in the genes of mice can be altered either by incorporating novel genes from another source or by deleting specific ones. Transgenic mice can be created, which are out-wardly fairly normal, but contain chromosome 21 – for example, from Alzheimer patients. This gives neuroscientists a very useful tool for under-standing the cause, and perhaps moving towards a cure, of AD. Another approach has been to produce 'knock-out' mutants of mice in which a specific gene, involved in some specific behaviour, is deleted.

As the methods of genetic engineering are improved, more interesting possibilities will arise, which may enable the ultimate questions regarding the brain – memory, creativity, emotions – to be answered. It may even be possible to find medication (rather than stimulants like alcohol) that are specific for increasing attention, arousal or even love. It should, however, not be forgotten that genetic engineering in humans is pre-sently illegal, and that the human genome (genetic apparatus) consists of up to 100,000 genes, most of whose functions are not yet known.

For nearly a hundred years, X-rays have been used for studying broken bones. Using less damaging soft X-rays, a technique known as com-puterized axial tomography (CAT scans) was used to study the structure of soft tissues such as the brain. Nowadays, as we have seen, exciting new techniques for looking inside a working human brain have been developed. PET and fMRI have become working tools for neurology, psychiatry and neuroscience, and have almost eliminated the need for using animal models for studying higher cognitive functions – except occasionally in cats or monkeys. Even newer technologies are currently being developed and the possibilities for using state-of-the-art machines are being constantly extended. For instance, electroencephalography (EEG) has spawned MEG (magnetoencephalography), by means of which minute changes in magnetic fields, deep inside the human cortex, can be recorded and correlated with brain function by computer. As a result of all these techniques, some of which can now be combined, many kinds of map of the brain are now available and correlated with function.

Magnetic resonance imaging may soon be used to diagnose Alzheimer's disease in the early stages, which will increase the chances of its successful treatment by medication. The use of functional MRI is becoming routine for the study of cognitive functions in humans, so that details of the visual system, the subtleties of language and the pathways involved in the other senses are gradually being unravelled. Very recent research at Harvard and Stanford Universities using fMRI has identified specific brain regions involved in the memory for photographs. The neuro-scientists there claim that they can predict which photographs will be remembered and which forgotten. These techniques will surely be extended to dreaming and hypnosis, and even to imagination and creativity.

The study of memory is, of course, one of the major goals of research using non-invasive techniques. An example of this is the use of faster and faster computers to investigate mental processes. This includes the possibility of playing games, looking at the rotation of objects, and learning simple things. Computers now control robots and guide space craft, and can even play championship chess. A very fast computer based on joining a number of parallel systems (as indeed happens in the brain) was built by IBM. This computer, called 'Deep Blue', can examine all the possible alternatives to each chess move in a few minutes, and has finally been able to defeat the chess champion of the world, Gary Kasparov.

As generations of computers have succeeded one another, each faster and more ingenious than the previous one, a possibility has been raised that silicon chips could be integrated with living brain cells, the one complementing the other. This may be the ultimate solution to the metaphysical mind–brain problem, which has been with us ever since it was raised by Plato over 2000 years ago. Everyone nowadays knows, more or less, what a brain is and does, at least in mammals. However, the term 'mind' has a long and confusing history, both in the English language and in philosophy. The words, 'mind', 'brain' and 'memory' have often been used interchangeably – examples are 'bringing to mind', meaning recalling, and 'keeping in mind', for remembering. One witty distortion of the word was penned by Mark Twain, who wrote, 'I have a prodigious quantity of mind, it takes me as much as a week sometimes to make it up.' For philosophers, the word 'mind' means a hypothetical system for explaining cognitive function, whereas 'brain' represents the not yet entirely understood neurophysiological and neurochemical mechanisms, i.e. the mind is the brain at work.

The mind–brain debate has been intensified by the use of synonyms for 'mind', such as 'soul', 'psyche' and even 'the self'. There has also been a tendency to confuse the mind–brain problem with the brain–body problem, which actually means the causing of diseases by mental attitudes such as fear, anxiety, depression and stress. These psychosomatic diseases appear to operate by the interaction between the nervous, the hormonal and the immune systems.

About fifty years ago, the Oxford philosopher Gilbert Ryle, in his book *The Concept of Mind*, questioned the existence of a human soul – the ghost in the machine, as he called it. He was, in effect, attacking Descartes, the seventeenth-century philosopher and mathematician, who stated that 'when the soul [sic] wants to remember something … volition makes the pineal gland lean first to one side and then the other, thus driving the spirits towards different regions of the brain until they come to the one containing traces left by the object we want to remember'. Descartes then gave a long explanation of memory based on the flow of spirits through pores of various sizes in the brain.

Ryle and his materialist followers insisted that the mind, soul, psyche or consciousness did not exist – or if it did, it was the same as the brain. A new breed of philosophers has now arisen, called 'The New Mysterians', who think that consciousness is mysterious, hence the name, and that mind is somehow involved; some have suggested that the human race at present does not have the conceptual ability to understand this dilemma. They suggest that something extra exists – perhaps consciousness – to give a sense of purpose to the universe, involving a return to religion and a single God. These non-materialistic philosophers of today have produced elaborate theories based on ideas such as 'pandemonium' (competing theories), and are waiting patiently for the proponents of artificial intelligence (AI) to prove them wrong by producing an intelligent machine that thinks and feels. The debate is still unresolved.

Some say, cynically, that the split between mind and brain has been maintained artificially by philosophers to encourage arguments and make their presence felt. What we need is an understanding of the mechanism for complex mental processes that are in the realm of beliefs and desires. There is much to do, too, in order to understand human memory, but we have come a long way since St Basil the Great, Bishop of Caesarea (in Cappadocia) said, in the fourth century AD, 'Memory is the cabinet of the imagination, the treasury of reason, the registry of conscience, and the council chamber of thought.'

As we get nearer and nearer to elucidating the various forms of memory, and to understanding forgetting, reasoning, conscience and imagination by using combinations of new techniques and concepts, we must remain sensitive to the real possibilities of manipulation of nervous tissue, and the control of people's thoughts and behaviour. By this I mean the dangers inherent in neural tissue transplants, 'bleach' and sophisticated pharmacology and genetic engineering in humans. However with foresight, wisdom and restraint there is no doubt that the future of research on memory will be very, very interesting.

GLOSSARY

acetylcholine an important neurotransmitter essential for memory processing.

action potential a sudden change in electric potential that travels down the neural axon; the bioelectrical method of neural transmission.

Alzheimer's disease (AD) a progressive, degenerative disease of the central nervous system that leads to severe dementia (loss of memory); once called senile dementia.

amnesia memory loss, frequently the result of brain injury.

animal models the use of animals (rats or monkeys), birds (chicks) or more primitive organisms (fruit flies, aplysia or octupuses), for the study of certain aspects of human biology and behaviour.

aphasia loss of the ability to use spoken language, often following brain injury.

aplysia sea-hare, a marine invertebrate the size of a small orange, used extensively as an animal model of behaviour, since it has only a few ten thousands of neural cells in its nervous system.

artificial intelligence (AI) the branch of computer science that attempts to develop computer programs capable of performing difficult cognitive tasks; it may help in understanding how the real brain works.

attention the ability to select part of incoming sensory information for further processing; also mental effort or concentration.

auditory sensory memory the system that holds the first few seconds of auditory (sound) information.

axons single fibres or processes that transmit information from one neuron to the next across a synapse.

blood–brain barrier (BBB) an extended 'barrier', formed by special cells lining the blood capillaries in the brain, which prevents any substances not essential for function from entering.

catecholamines important neurotransmitters such as dopamine and norepinephrine, involved in attention, movement, mood, etc.

central nervous system (CNS) the brain and spinal cord.

cerebral blood flow (CBF) the flow of blood through capillaries inside and around the brain, supplying oxygen and nutrients to the cells.

cerebellum part of the brain located at the back of the head, involved mainly in balance, motor co-ordination, breathing, etc.

chunking the grouping of items to facilitate memory processing.

cognitive science the study of the acquisition and use of knowledge, including AI, psychology, philosophy, anthropology, neuroscience and education.

conditioning the set of concepts or methods that specify the conditions under which some forms of learning take place.

consciousness awareness of one's own mental processes.

consolidation change in structure of memory that occurs with the passage of time after learning (different from forgetting); transition from short-term to long-term memory.

cortex (cerebral) outer layers of cells in avian and mammalian brains, involved in sensory and cognitive functions, including memory (divided into frontal, motor, visual, etc. cortices).

cue a trigger for mental and other behavioural processes.

declarative memory memory that can be described, i.e. put into spoken words.

dementia a neurological condition in which intellectual functions (including memory) are lost, usually accompanied by personality changes.

dendrite richly branched, tree-like processes, attached to neurons, which receive and carry information from other neurons.

dopamine (DA) an important neurotransmitter involved in attention, movement and mood.

drosophila melanogaster fruit flies with many mutants, used for the study of simple forms of learning and memory.

echoic memory short-lived, acoustic memory, used for locating sources of sounds.

electroencephalogram (EEG) a record of changes in electrical potential in the brain, usually measured by electrodes attached to the skull.

emotions various enjoyable or distressing mental states.

engram a hypothetical memory trace (or location) in the brain.

episodic memory conscious recollection of personal events or dates in the past.

forgetting the loss of ability to recall or recognize what was previously learned or identified.

free recall memory without specific cues.

functional magnetic resonance imaging (fMRI) a technique based on nuclear magnetic resonance, used for correlating maps of the brain (and other organs) with functions such as learning, seeing and dreaming.

hippocampus a small structure in mammalian brains, looking like a sea-horse, central to memory processing.

hypnosis a technique of inducing deep relaxation by suggesting sleep, etc; differs from sleep in that the subject can still respond to suggestions and commands.

iconic memory short-lived visual memory.

implicit memory an unconscious form of memory that appears to operate independently of previous experience.

imprinting a phenomenon, almost specific to domesticated birds (chicks, geese), in which patterns of ambulatory behaviour are set by early experience; it also occurs in infants learning to smile in response to their mother.

incidental learning behaviour learned apparently without specific attention.

ischemia a temporary lack of blood supply (oxygen) to an organ, such as the brain.

learning relatively permanent changes in behaviour or knowledge as a result of experience or reinforcement.

lesions cuts in, or removal of, specific parts of the brain, used for correlating brain structure and function.

long-term memory (LTM) a general term for information that has been well processed and integrated into the store of knowledge; it lasts longer than a few minutes and there are apparently a number of such systems working in parallel.

long-term potentiation (LTP) change in synaptic efficiency lasting some weeks, caused by brief, high-frequency electrical stimulation of the hippocampus, considered to be a model for memory.

mnemonics special techniques for improving memory.

neuron excitable nerve cells that are the basic components of the nervous system; together with other cells, collectively known as glia, and blood capillaries, they provide the bulk of the central nervous system.

neuropeptides short chains of amino acids that can act either as neurotransmitters or as hormones.

neurotransmitters molecules involved in the relay of nerve impulses from one neuron to another (or to a muscle) across the synaptic gap.

perception the acquisition of information from the environment by means of the senses, and its transformation into experiences of objects, events, etc.

positron emission tomography (PET) a technique, using short-lived radio-isotopes, for creating maps of the brain that can be correlated with areas where neuronal activity is higher, and blood flow is faster, it is used for pinpointing areas of altered activity or metabolism, or neural damage.

procedural memory memory for complex activities that do not require conscious thought, i.e. highly automatized.

processes slender extensions from neurons, connecting one to another; they consist of axons and dendrites.

recall reproduction of information (usually visual or verbal) from memory; differs from recognition and retrieval.

recognition awareness of an object or event previously seen, experienced or learned, different from and usually easier than recall.

rehearsal the repetitive review of material previously learned and 'held' in short-term memory.

retrieval a general term for recalling information from memory.

semantic memory memory necessary for the use of language.

serotonin (5HT) a neurotransmitter involved in sleep, depression, etc.

short-term memory (STM) a term that used to be used for memory processing of events occurring during the last few seconds or minutes; also called working memory, it is limited to seven or so items at any one time, and requires constant rehearsal.

state-dependent memory memory dependent on physical or psychological state (mood, pain, drugs, alcohol, etc.), under the influence of which learning occurred.

stress an acute or chronic state of psychological tension caused by various pressures.

synapse the junction between neurons (or neurons and muscles), where neurotransmitters control activity in the nervous system.

synaptic gap the gap between the outer membranes of two neurons, across which neurotransmitters diffuse; the major method of control in the nervous system.

Wechsler Adult Intelligence Scale (WAIS) the best-known and widely used test for assessing general intellectual ability in adults.

Wechsler Memory Scale (WMS) a widely used pencil-and-paper test for loss of memory or dementia in adults, used together with WAIS.

working memory a memory system more general than, and used instead of, short-term memory for mental processes taking a few seconds or minutes.

BIBLIOGRAPHY

Baddeley, Alan, *Your Memory: A User's Guide*, Penguin (1992).

Bloom, Floyd, Lazerson, Arlyne, and Hofstadter, Laura, *Brain, Mind and Behavior*, W. H. Freeman & Co. (1988).

Cohen, David, *The Secret Language of the Mind*, Chronicle Books, San Francisco (1966).

Dudai, Yadin, *The Neurobiology of Memory: Concepts, Findings, Trends*, Oxford University Press (1989).

Greenfield, Susan E. (ed.) *Your Mind Explained*, Cassell (1996).

Greenfield, Susan E., *The Human Brain: A Guided Tour*, Weidenfeld & Nicolson (1997).

Posner, Michael I. and Raichle, Marcus E., *Images of Mind*, W. H. Freeman & Co. (1994).

Rose, Steven, *The Making of Memory: From Molecules to Mind*, Bantam (1992).

Squire, Larry, *Memory and Brain*, Oxford University Press (1987).

Yates, Frances, *The Art of Memory*, Routledge & Kegan Paul (1966).

Index